Chinese Education
in Singapore

An untold story of
conflict and change

By Zhang Zhixiong

National Library Board, Singapore Cataloguing-in-Publication Data

Zhang, Zhixiong.
Chinese education in Singapore: an untold story of conflict and
change / Zhang Zhixiong. – Singapore: Pacific Media, c2016.

ISBN 978-981-09-9974-2 (paperback)

1. Chinese – Education – Government policy – Singapore – History –
20th century.   2. Chinese – Education – Political aspects – Singapore – History – 20th century.   3. Chinese language – Government
policy – Singapore – History – 20th century.   4. Schools, Chinese
– Government policy – Singapore – History – 20th century.

DDC 371.0095957 – dc23

OCN 952971290

For the memory of the Hylam kids,
Leonard and Johnny

CONTENTS

• • • • • • • • • • •

INTRODUCTION

Singapore is not a part of China. It is a former British colony eighty-five miles north of the equator. Although its population is barely more than five million people (in 2014), its smartest kids now rank among the best in International Mathematical Olympiads. And its average fifteen-year-old students had topped the Programme for International Student Assessment (PISA), a worldwide study by the Organization for Economic Co-operation and Development (OECD). (Lately, Singapore has lost its pole position for PISA to Shanghai though.)

What about its past? As you turn the pages of this book, you will find out how its youths were taught in this island of less than 300 square miles. (It is still tiny despite aggressive reclamation.)

Chapter 1

• • • • • • • • • •

THE MIGRANT PROTAGONISTS
Heroes, villains, and others

Once upon a time, the old people say, there was in Singapore an economic ladder, whose rungs were set so far apart by family and clan loyalties that social mobility was limited. Status groups were characterized by language, with the Hokkien at the top of the pecking order, followed by the Teochew, and then the Cantonese. That is why the ladder was scaled with greater ease by those with an education in the English language.

(Both Hokkien and Teochew people speak Southern-mĭn Chinese, or Mĭnnán.)

The Hokkien people built and captained ships; they possessed the capital from fortunes made over centuries; and they have knowledge and experience of trading in Southeast Asia, gained over hundreds of years. Since the thirteenth century, they carried out their commerce in Southeast Asia with the patronage of the Song, Yuan, Ming, and Qing emperors. When the Ming emperors closed the kingdom and forbade all but official contact with foreigners, they trafficked illegally. The Kangxi Emperor of the Qing dynasty, whose reign greatly increased the wealth of China, granted those from Xiamen (Amoy) the privilege of foreign trade.

During the early eighteenth century, "tea" was pronounced as "tey" in English, rhyming with "obey." To this day, the word is still pronounced as "tey" in Irish, and in the Xiamen dialect.[1]

The Cantonese were conversely ravaged by wars and wasted by opium addiction. They were lured by promises of gold in California, but recruited to build the Transcontinental Railroad. From the mining fields of the Gold Coast, Australia, to the fur-trading outposts of Nootka Sound, Canada, most Chinese indentured laborers were men from Guangdong Province. They were exempted from the migration ban because the Treaty of Nanjing compelled the Qing Government to legalize the coolie trade.

But since women and children were not granted immunity from punishment if they migrate, their families were forced to stay back. Forsaken by destitution, many Cantonese women left home, finding employment at houses of ill-repute in foreign enclaves, such as Hong Kong or Shanghai.[2]

After the Second Opium War, the Qing prohibition on migration could only be loosely enforced in practice. But Washington and Wellington and the other governments of the Western world impeded female immigration by legislation and tax.

- The United States enacted the Page Act in 1875, prohibiting the entry of "cheap Chinese labor and immoral Chinese women." But to protect the system of monogamous marriages, they imposed the law only on female immigration. Chinese wives could enter the country only after the Second World War.
- New Zealand introduced a "poll tax" of £10 in 1881. It was increased to £100 in 1896. The tax made it difficult for Chinese men to bring their wives, who were incapacitated by bound feet. When help was required, grown-up sons, brothers, and nephews were sent in their place. (Wives and children were let in only at the outbreak of the Second World War, as refugees.)

The emperor put an end to the migration prohibition in 1893. So, the debauchery moved from the treaty ports of China to the ports of trade in Southeast Asia, including Singapore[3].

Traffickers abused the xùbì system for commercial gain, selling girls into prostitution. More than three thousand yuèjì, or Cantonese prostitutes, were working at some 200 registered brothels in 1898. Six hundred more prostitutes, mainly Teochew, were at 150 Chinese brothels that were unregistered.[4]

At that time, there were only about 150,000[5] Chinese in Singapore. Men, mostly.

(Brothels were registered by the Chinese Protectorate, after it was assigned to check prostitutes for venereal diseases.)

The Xùbì system

A Xùbì's road to ruin was paved with good intentions. As a child of the poor, she was owned by the wealthy, who bought her to do domestic labor. After puberty, she may become a concubine of her master, or be married off for a dowry, or be given away in marriage, as a daughter of her master.

But these enslaved servants were often bought and re-sold as chattel. They were taken far away from their communities, where traditional social checks could prevent abuses.

The Cantonese term for enslaved servant is *Nou Pei*, or *núbì* in Mandarin, and the Hokkien term is *Char Boh Kan*.

But the Cantonese used the word *mui-tsai* to describe victims of child sex trafficking. *Mui-tsai* is pronounced as *muē-á* or *bē-á* in Mǐnnán. It simply means a young girl to the Mǐnnán Chinese, who even use it as an adoring form of address for the younger girls in the family. Destitute Cantonese parents, in their hardest hours of grief, were comforted by the folly that their daughters were sold for adoption into wealthy, benevolent homes in Shantou (Swatow).

The other term that may be helpful for understanding language differences is "a young girl." It is *sai-lou-neoi* in

11

Cantonese and *xiǎo-nǔ-hái* in Mandarin. The written characters for both Chinese words are different.

(In 1949, the communist government abolished the practice of keeping xùbì.)

Bāngpài means "gang" or "faction." Its contraction, *bāng*, is commonly used and has more than one meaning. When used as a verb, the short form means "help." But when used as a noun, it means "group" or "gang" or "clique" or "party" or "secret society."

The Hakka

Only the Hakka Chinese had two bāng in the Singapore Chinese Chamber of Commerce, according to its 1959 constitution. In all likelihood, the Dabu bāng represented only those from Chaozhou Prefecture; and the Meixian bāng, Jiaying Prefecture. That left out the Hakka Chinese from Fujian Province, whose wealth aroused the envy of their kinsmen, and the hicks from upcountry Guangdong prefectures, who made engaging history.

The Larut Wars

In the Perak Sultanate (see Fig 1 for locator map), some migrants from Guangdong Province in China joined the Yìxīng Company, which was the Malayan offshoot of the Heaven and Earth Society. The company was also known as the Sì-xiàn Company, or the company of four counties: Xinning, Gugang, Huizhou, Zhaoqing.[6]

Others from the same province joined the Hǎishān Company. But they were natives of Zengcheng, Panyu, Shunde, Nanhai, and Dongguan counties. The rival company was also known as the Wǔ-xiàn Company, or the company of five counties.[7]

The leaders of the Yìxīng Company were from Huizhou prefecture, whose natives speak a Hakka dialect that is influenced by Cantonese. And, because they were numerically the most dominant members of the Hǎishān Company, the Hakka also led the rival company, but they were from Zengcheng County.[8]

Tin deposits were discovered in Larut, a desolated swamp between the Perak River watershed and the sea. The Yìxīng Company worked its mines at Klian Bahru, while the Hǎishān based themselves in Klian Pauh.

A series of four wars, which the two companies fought from 1861 to 1874, for the control of mines in the district was known as the Larut Wars.

Pronunciation table for the various Chinese dialects

Mandarin	Hokkien	Cantonese	Hakka
Yìxīng Company	Ghee Hin Kongsi	Ji-hing Gung-si	Ngi-hin Gung-sii

Hǎishān Company	Hai San Kongsi	Hoi-saan Gung-si	Hoi-san Gung-sii
Sì-xiàn Company	Si-kuan Kongsi	Sei-jyun Gung-si	Xi-rhen Gung-sii
Wǔ-xiàn Company	Go-kuan Kongsi	Ng-jyun Gung-si	Ng-rhen Gung-sii

The British, who seemingly gathered intelligence not on the ground in Perak but from the Peranakans on Penang Island, used the Hokkien pronunciation in their dispatches about the Larut Wars. Shaken by violence and stirred by necessity, the Englishmen foisted the Pangkor Treaty upon the sultanate in 1874, giving James Birch a license to instill British policies. After mixing business with girls and thrills, he was killed the next year, without his clothes on, but it's probably not what you think. The first British Resident in Perak outlawed slavery in the sultanate, and he was assassinated after he unwittingly insulted the sultan by sheltering his slave girls.

(By the way, I have decided to break with the past and use the Mandarin pronunciation.)

The Hǎishān drove the Yìxīng out of Klian Bahru in the first war. The Governor of Straits Settlements intervened and got the Malay headman who was the administrator of Larut to compensate the Yìxīng.[9]

During the second war, the leader of the Yìxīng Company was captured and executed. Most Huizhou migrants gave up Larut, moving to the mines in Sungai Besi, Selangor, and leaving the leadership of the Yìxīng Company for the members from Xinning.[10]

At first, the Xinning Chinese were not members of the Yìxīng Company. They were members of Héhé Society (Ho Hap Seah). Their leader had set up the society in Penang during the early eighteen-sixties. He appointed one member to be a faction chief of the Yìxīng Company in Larut, and he sent another as replacement after the first faction chief was killed by the Hǎishān.[11]

The second faction chief was also a Xinning Chinese, and he was likely to become the next leader of Héhé Society, which had only 2,000 members. The Hǎishān Company had 10,000 members. So, the society mobilized the fellowship. A ring of alliances was struck among members of: the Héhé Society, who may have been Taishanese; the Yìxīng Company in Penang, who were Teochew and Cantonese; the Yìxīng Company from the Kerian District, who were Teochew; and the remnant Yìxīng Company in Larut.[12] As a side note, the Teochew Chinese pronounce Yìxīng as Ngee-heng, and the Taishanese pronounce it as Ni-hein.

The Penang Hǎishān Company assimilated the Huásheng (Wah Sang) Society to bolster itself. Their allies, the wealthy Jiàndé (Kian Tek) Society, made up in arms for whatever they lacked in numbers.

15

Members of Jiàndé Society were Hokkiens of Zhang-zhou descent. Most were born in Penang; the rest, natu-ralized British subjects.[13] A number were licensed to sell weapons and gunpowder.[14]

The other triads consisted wholly of China-born mi-grants[15], though several living in Penang may also have been naturalized British subjects[16].

The war also spilled over into Penang between the sec-ond and the third war. In the Penang Riots of 1867, the Penang branch of the Yìxīng Company fought the Jiàndé Society, who were allies of the Hǎishān Company. This nine-day battle in Georgetown was a half-time show, put up by the Yìxīng and Hǎishān affiliates to keep British spectators in their seats.

The First Larut War had divided a Hakka association in Penang. Members of Eng Tai Association were from Yongding (Eng Teng) County and Dabu (Tai Pu) District. The Yongding Hakka aligned themselves with the Penang Hokkien merchants, since their county is in Fujian Prov-ince. The Dabu Hakka and the Teochew swore brother-hood at the Hanjiang Ancestral Temple in 1864. Poit-ip means "eight districts" in Teochew, and it referred to the Mǐnnán-speaking districts of Teochew prefecture. Two other districts in the prefecture, Dabu and Fengshun (Hongsun) were Hakka-speaking. At the community tem-ple where the Penang Teochew Association would later be founded, they swore an oath of nine-district brother-hood, signifying that they accepted the migrants from Dabu as ga-gi-nang, or "one of the family."[17]

The chaos from the incessant warfare compelled the sultan to place Perak under British protection. The British and the local Malay chiefs signed the Pangkor Treaty, resolving the Perak succession dispute and ending the war between the secret societies. Among the signatories were the heads of the Hǎishān and Yìxīng Companies. Héhé Society's second faction chief signed the agreement on behalf of the Yìxīng Company.

Larut was joined with two other districts, Matang and Selama. The enlarged area was then divided into two. Klian Bahru, which means "new mines" in Malay, was renamed Kamunting and leased to the Yìxīng Company. Klian Pauh, which means "mango mines" in Malay, was renamed Taiping and set aside for the Hǎishān Company.

In Mandarin, *tài* means "great", and *píng*, "peace." In Mǐnnán, Hakka, and Yuè (Cantonese), the pronunciations are roughly the same.

The Hainanese

Chinese women were forbidden to leave China, so men from Hainan Island, which was then a part of Guangdong Province, left home for Singapore and sought employment in European households as menservants and cooks. Although many were middle-agers with children of their own, these domestic coolies were called houseboys and cookboys, in the paternalistic language of the colonizers. A few were even twice the age of their employers, but with the front of their heads shaven and the back braided in long, black pigtails, these men were cast as "boys" who were docile and obedient, handy and efficient.

A population census, taken in 1881, found 12,586 men and 318 women working as domestic servants in Singapore.[18] The first Chinese Protector, William Pickering, once stated that wealthy Chinese towkays kept, in their homes, large numbers of women who were called servants, out of "a sense of delicacy." Many female domestic workers were Hokkien girls and Javanese women, discreetly purchased.[19]

The second last emperor of China, Guangxu, abrogated the migration prohibition in 1893, and that encouraged women to leave China. But most worked at houses with red doors, and they were not maidservants. Chinese women found it hard to take up heavy domestic work because their feet were bounded.

For decades, chain migration had moderated this replacement. To cement their status as Singapore's preferred housekeepers, the Hainanese brought their relatives and clansmen into the occupation. Menservants were only replaced in significant numbers by maidservants, after Hainanese men cut their queues, and Cantonese women stopped binding their feet.

A few years after cutting off their waist-long, braided pigtails and shortly after the First World War, the menservants saw their sons organizing the first trade unions in Singapore. Several youngsters were graduates from the Whampoa Military and Political College in Guangzhou. They radicalized the Guomindang in Singapore, turning night schools into party branches, spreading anti-capitalist, anti-imperialist ideas to students and party members.[20]

But meanwhile, as they were being discharged from employment at European households, the menservants became practitioners of the three blades – razors, scissors, cleavers – or more commonly known as the barber, the tailor, and the chicken-rice seller.

Hainanese parents and their children may have called each other bo-vad-di. These invectives are a pair of Hainanese homophones for the Chinese words meaning "reckless" and "illiterate." (Please see glossary for Chinese characters.)

In any case, an article in the Straits Times advised "the younger Hainanese [to] devote their spare time to something less exciting than fulminations against imperialism, the Guomindang, and the established order of things in Malaya [or] they will find it somewhat difficult to earn a living in this country in the future."[21]

The other Cantonese women

The colonial government enacted the Immigration Restriction Ordinance in 1928, but did not enforce the law until a few years later. During the Great Depression, the colonial government expected a higher unemployment rate, so they set quotas and levied fees on Chinese coolie immigration from August 1930.[22] They suspended the law only in 1941, when the Pacific War started.

Because the sex ratio of Singapore was skewed, the British authorities sought to rectify it by excluding women and children from the quota. That made it possible for women to replace men as laborers, toiling in construction sites. These women, with no building skills for other work, carried bricks and sand. They donned navy-blue work-shirts and wore scarves on the head, scarves that were folded to look like rectangular roofs, shading their heads and faces from the sun.

The women also wore these headgears to commemorate Wang Chaoyun, a well-known courtesan in the West Lake area of Hangzhou prefecture. At twelve, she was redeemed by the prefect of Suzhou during the Song Dynasty. She later became the concubine of her master. As she was unlettered, she taught herself to read, and became the most famous of his companions. Her husband, one of the greatest poets of his time, dedicated a number of his poems to her, and his friend, another famous poet, wrote a poem praising her beauty and lovely voice. After she died, her husband did not get married again. The female construction workers believed she was the first woman to wear scarves in that manner.[23]

The scarves were of varying colors at first. But as more female laborers worked on construction sites, their managers color-coded these headgears to help communication. Hakka women wore blue. Those from Qingyuan wore light blue. And since they formed the majority, those from Sanshui were given the opportunity to wear red, the auspicious color found on almost everything during Chinese New Year and also on the cover of this book.[24]

The unskilled female workers from Sìyì also dressed the same way. But they put on black headgears and worked as dock laborers.[25]

(Note: Sanshui is pronounced as Samsui in Cantonese. Sìyì is pronounced as Sze Yup in Cantonese, and it means four districts, referring to Taishan (Toisan), Xinhui, Kaiping, and Enping.)

A difference of opinion

The late communist guerrilla leader in Malaya had Fuzhou ancestry. When recounting his childhood days at Sitiawan, Chin Peng said he conversed mostly in Hokkien, but spoke with his mother in her Amoy dialect.[26] (Amoy is pronounced as Xiamen in Mandarin.)

But the Xiamen Chinese in Singapore believed that the Hokkien language was theirs, and they held the contrary notion that the dialect spoken at Sitiawan was Hokchew. (Hokchew is pronounced as Fuzhou in Mandarin.)

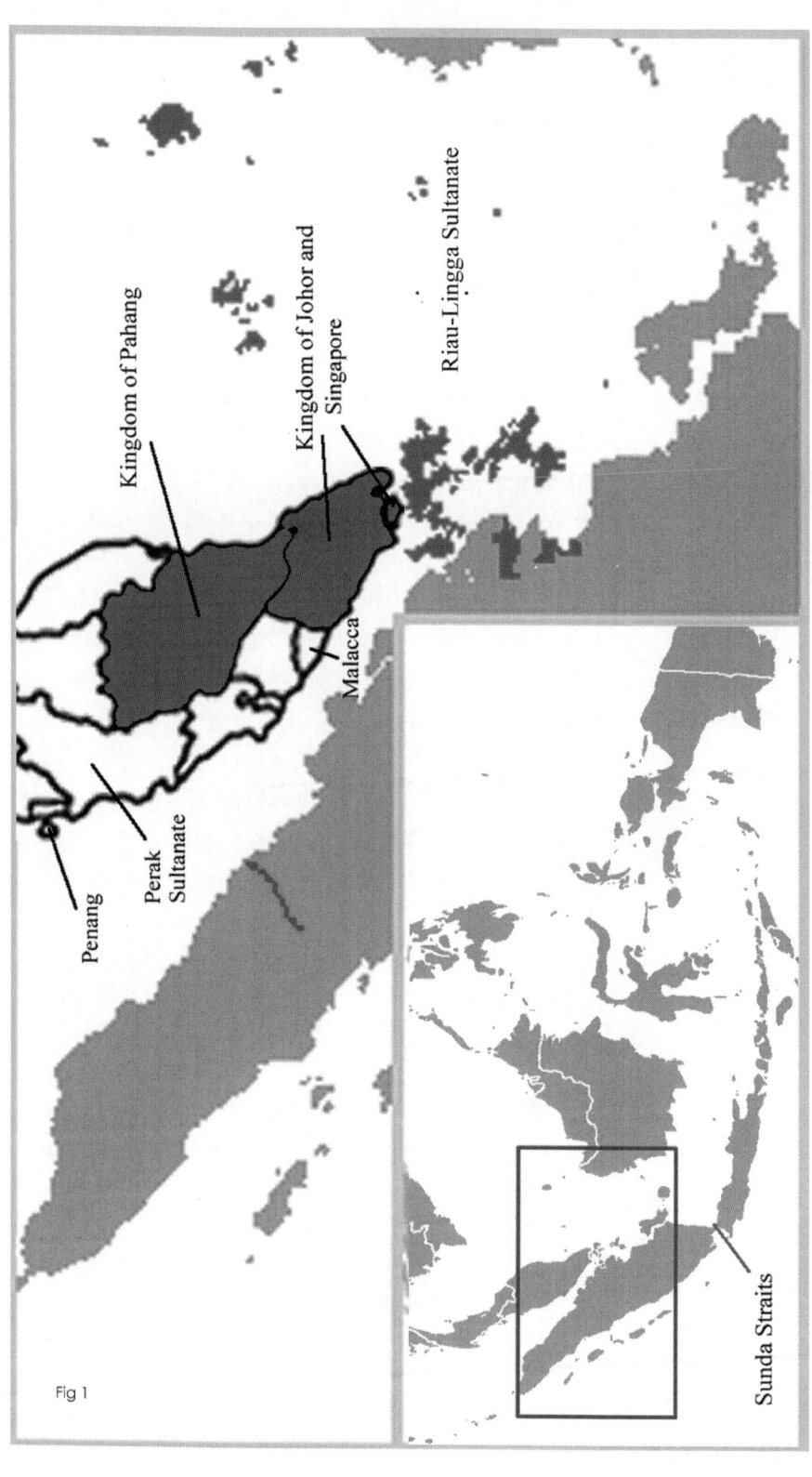

Fig 1

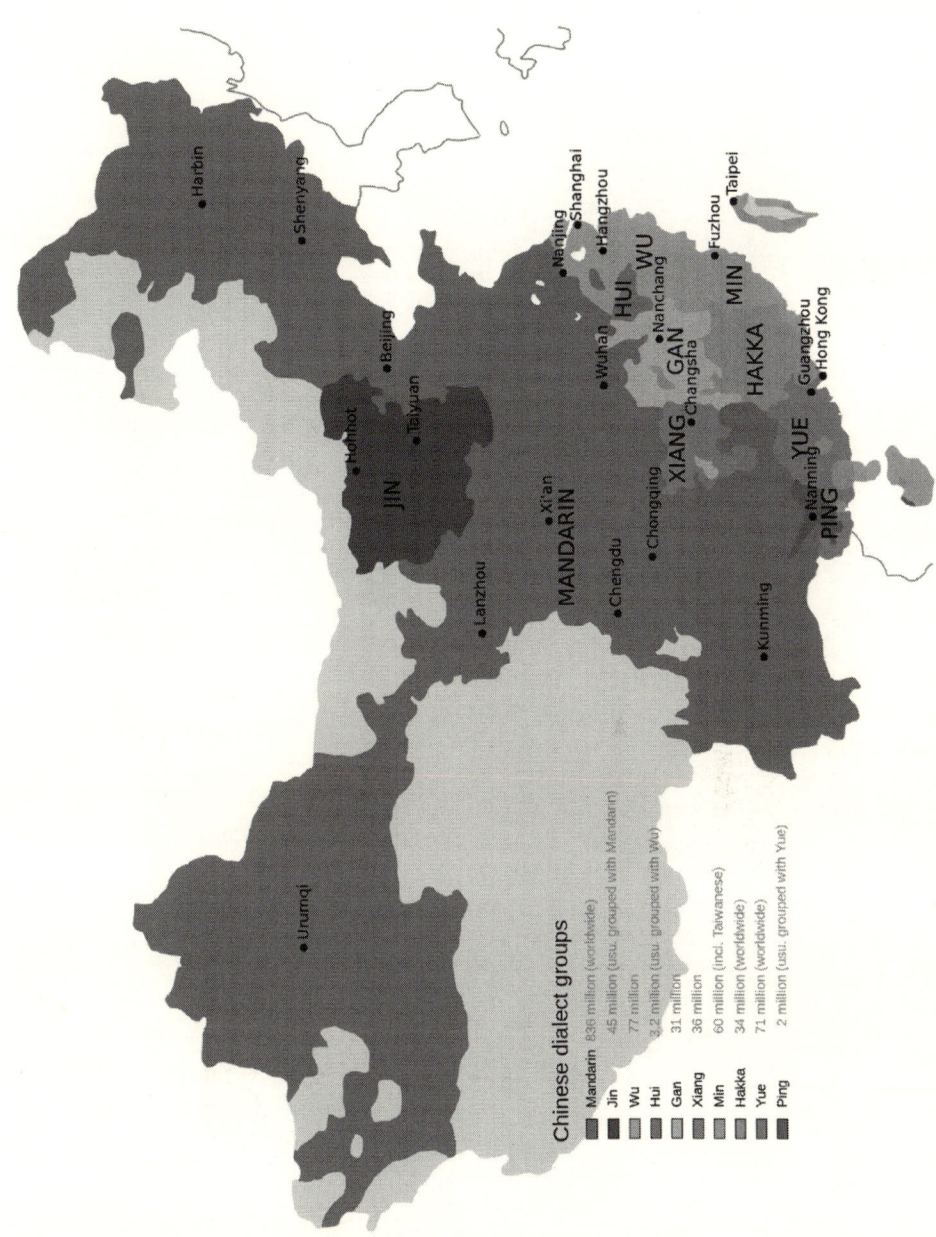

Fig 2 (See footnote 28 for image credit and color-image url.)

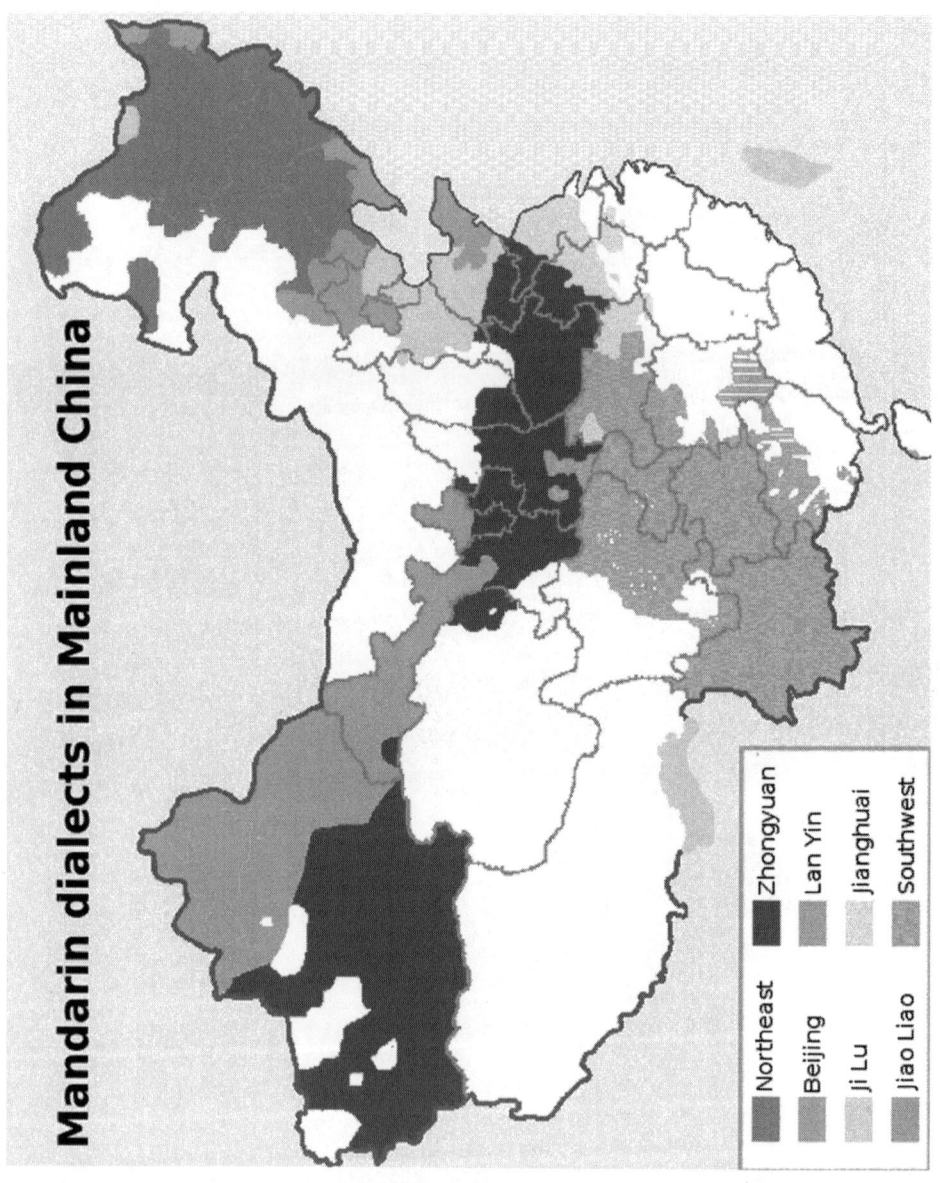

Mandarin dialects in Mainland China

Legend:
- Northeast
- Beijing
- Ji Lu
- Jiao Liao
- Zhongyuan
- Lan Yin
- Jianghuai
- Southwest

Fig 3 (See footnote 30 for image credit and color-image url.)

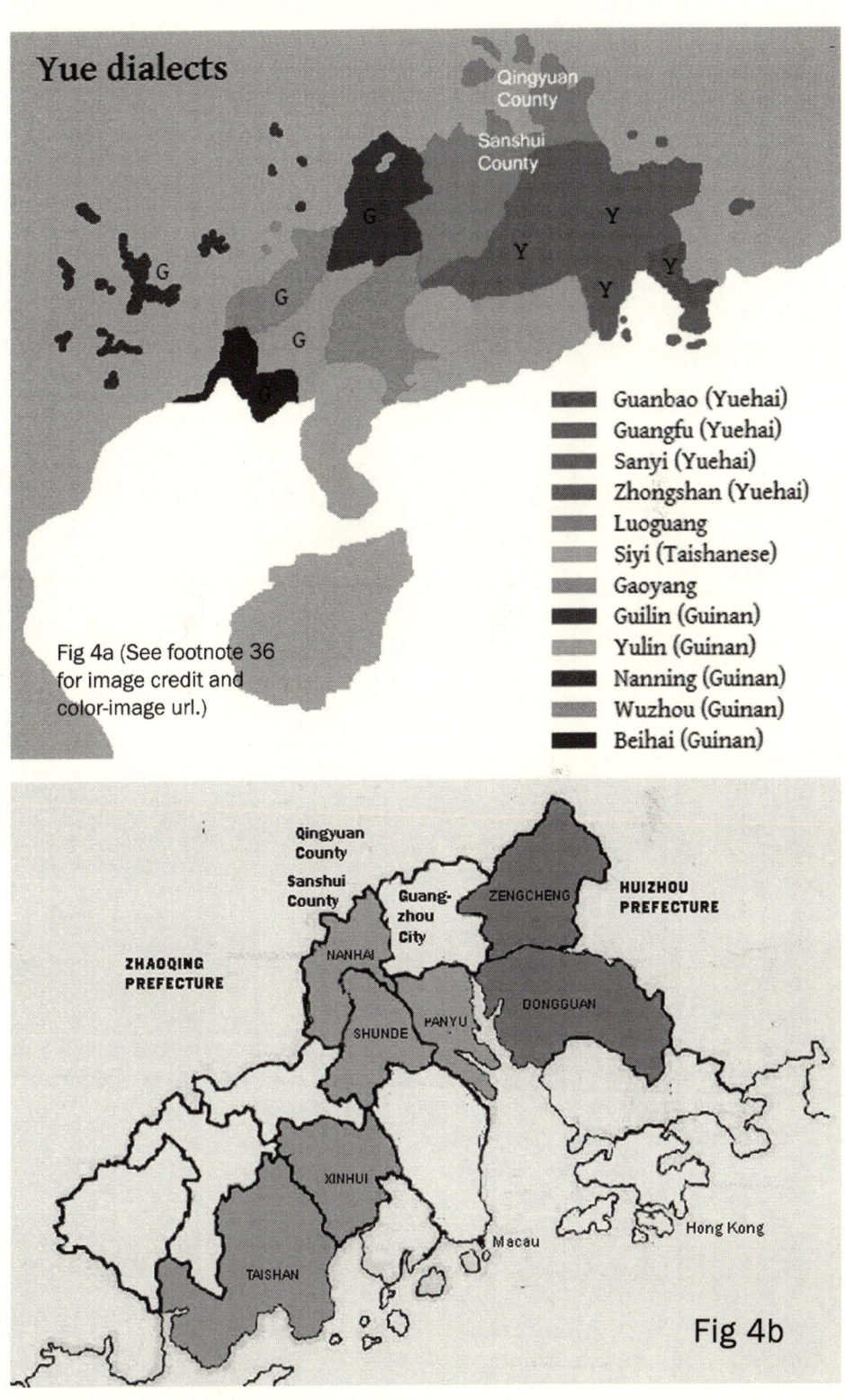

Yue dialects

Qingyuan County

Sanshui County

G
G
G
G

Y
Y
Y
Y

Legend:
- Guanbao (Yuehai)
- Guangfu (Yuehai)
- Sanyi (Yuehai)
- Zhongshan (Yuehai)
- Luoguang
- Siyi (Taishanese)
- Gaoyang
- Guilin (Guinan)
- Yulin (Guinan)
- Nanning (Guinan)
- Wuzhou (Guinan)
- Beihai (Guinan)

Fig 4a (See footnote 36 for image credit and color-image url.)

Qingyuan County

Sanshui County

ZHAOQING PREFECTURE

Guang-zhou City

NANHAI

SHUNDE

PANYU

ZENGCHENG

HUIZHOU PREFECTURE

DONGGUAN

XINHUI

TAISHAN

Macau

Hong Kong

Fig 4b

Fig 3

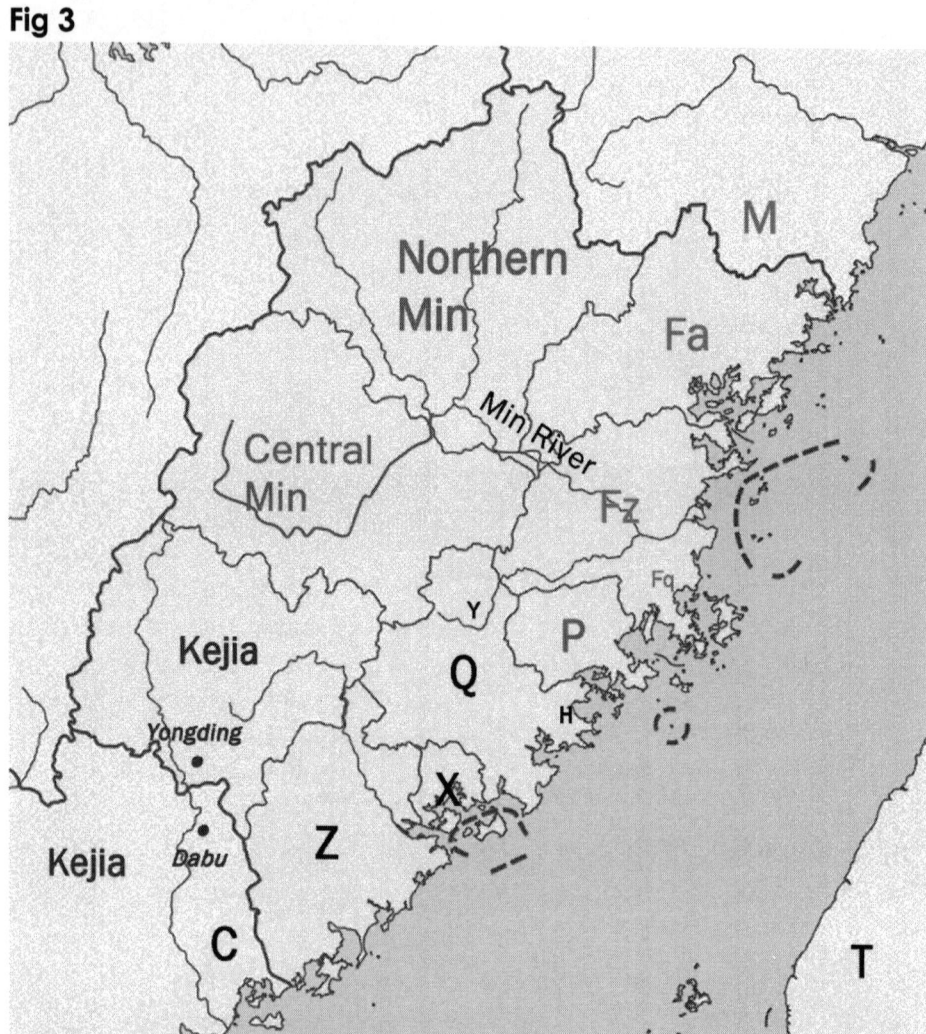

Number of pupils at school in Singapore

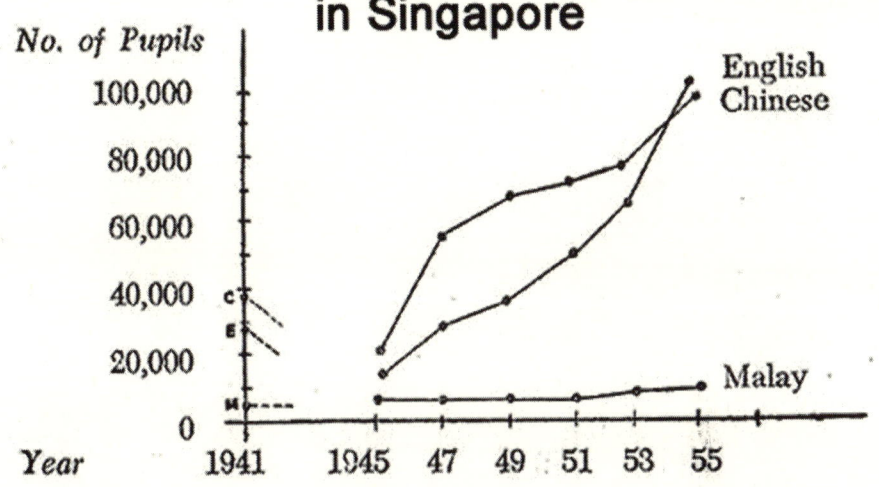

No. of Pupils

100,000							English
80,000							Chinese
60,000							
40,000							
20,000							Malay
0							

Year 1941 1945 47 49 51 53 55

Fig 6

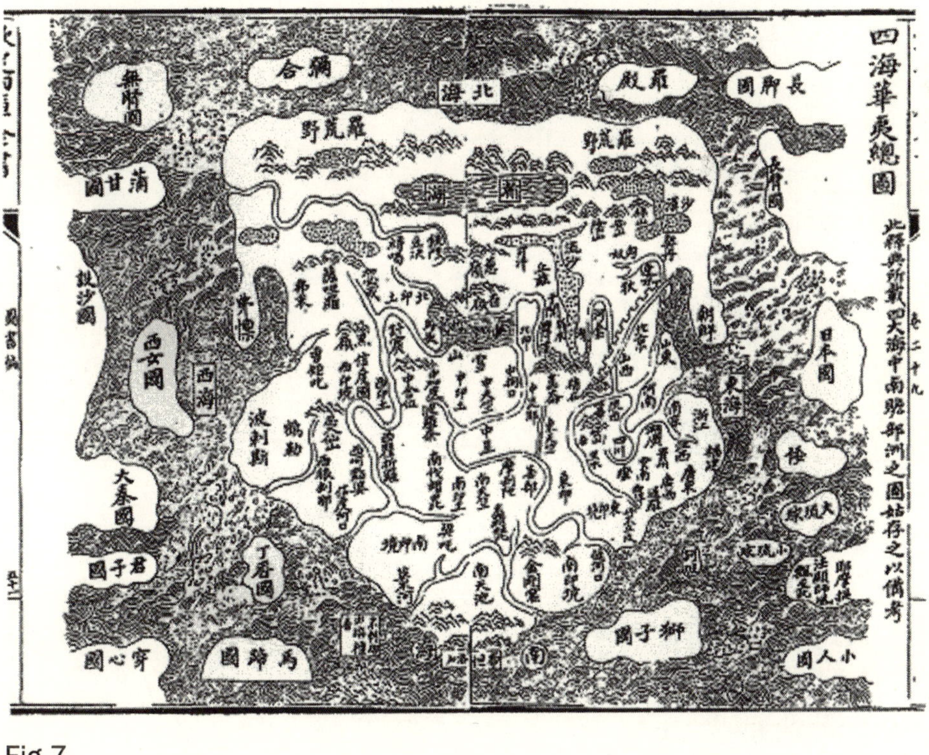

四海華夷總圖

此釋典所載天海中南贍部洲之圖姑存之以備考

Fig 7

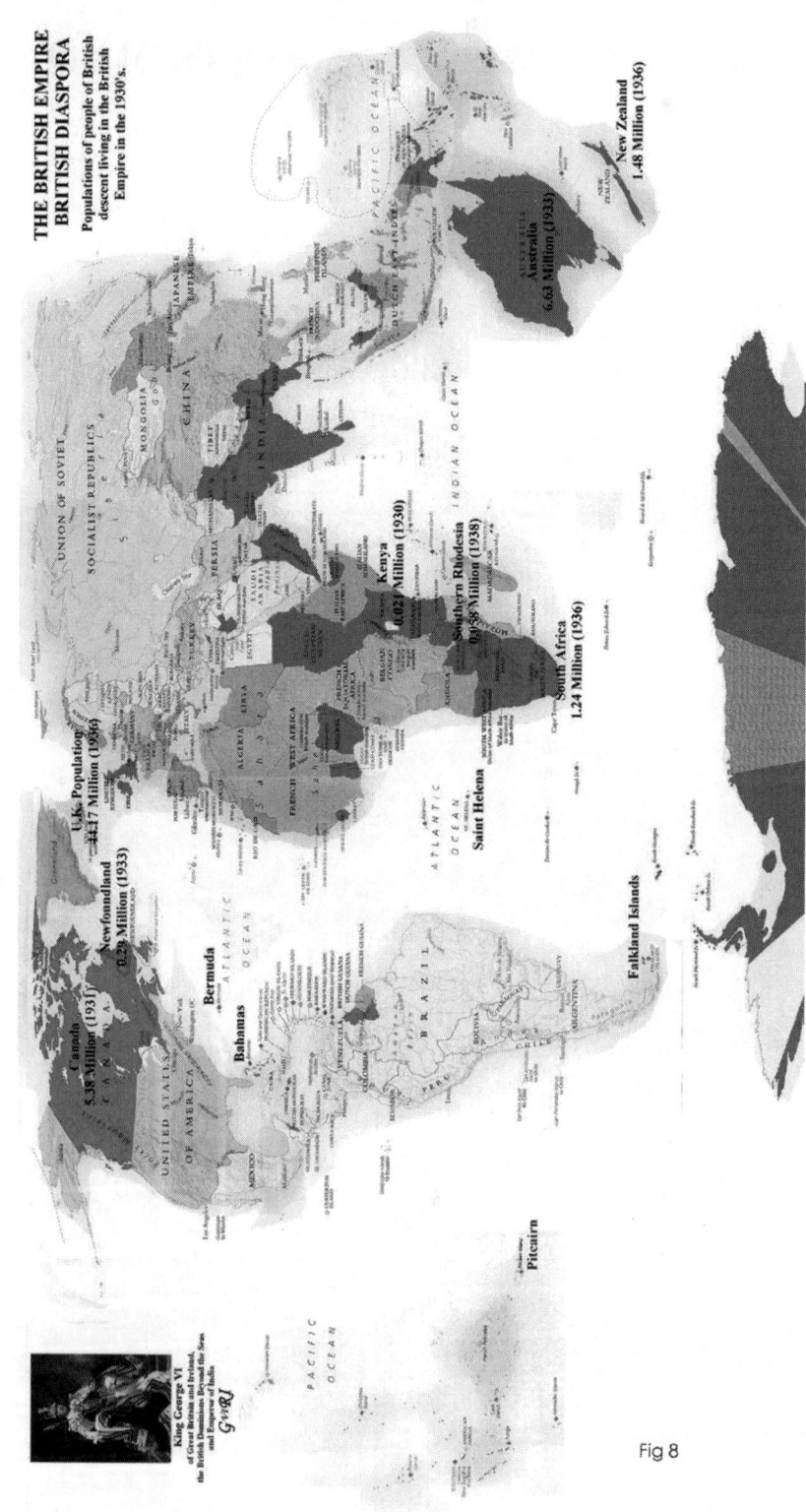

THE BRITISH EMPIRE
BRITISH DIASPORA

Populations of people of British descent living in the British Empire in the 1930's.

New Zealand
1.48 Million (1936)

Australia
6.63 Million (1933)

Kenya
0.02 Million (1930)

Southern Rhodesia
0.58 Million (1938)

South Africa
1.24 Million (1936)

Saint Helena

Falkland Islands

U.K. Population
44.17 Million (1936)

Newfoundland
0.29 Million (1933)

Canada
5.38 Million (1931)

Bermuda

Bahamas

Pitcairn

King George VI
of Great Britain and Ireland,
the British Dominions Beyond the Seas
and Emperor of India
G VI R J

Fig 8

Exploring links between education policy and migration

Changes in education policy

1979: Min.grade of C6 for English as a first language (at Grade 10) and E8 for 2nd language needed for admission into pre-university (at Grade 11).

1980: 2nd language requirement for pre-U tightened to D7. Students were streamed into Normal, Extended, or Monolingual classes at primary 4 (or Grade 4).

1981: Min. grade D7 needed in 2nd language for admission into NUS, and 2nd language grades were included in the admission score calculation.

1988: ACS, SJI, and Chinese High School became independent. With greater flexibility in admitting boys, these schools allow for a more diverse range of student achievements and talents.

1989: MGS and SCGS became independent, acknowledging that girls have achievements and talents in many different areas too.

1992: Singapore Math revised to emphasize problem solving.

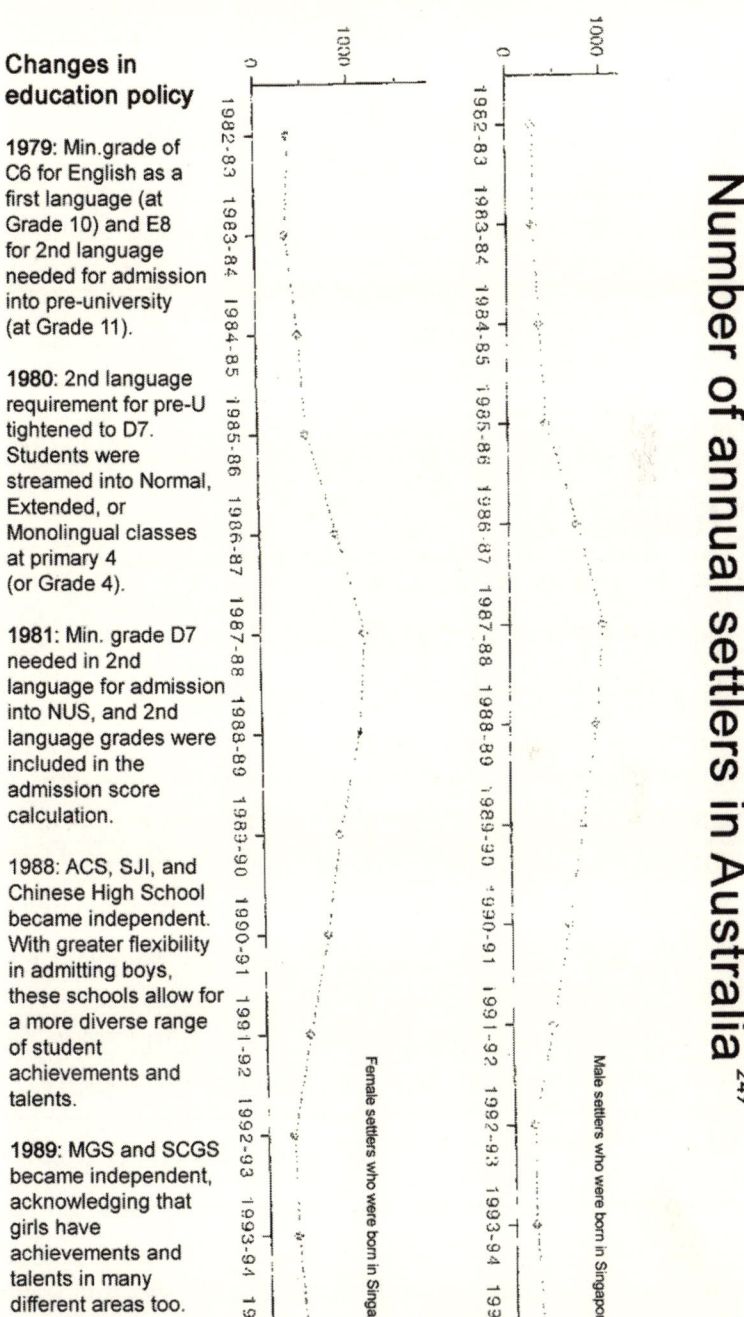

Number of annual settlers in Australia 249

Female settlers who were born in Singapore

Male settlers who were born in Singapore

Fig 9

Chapter 2

● ● ● ● ● ● ● ● ● ●

CHINESE LANGUAGES
How the protagonists talked

Bāng fought bāng. Clan fought clan. Back in 1854, for example, the Hokkien and the Teochew Chinese fought each other in Singapore, leaving 500 dead and some 300 homes destroyed in at least ten days of fighting. The riot gave rise to a new Teochew secret society, the Yìfú (Ghee Hock) Company.[27]

"Hokkien" is the Mǐnnán name for Fujian Province in China, and "Teochew", for Chaozhou Prefecture in the Qing Empire.

Chinese migrants who moved into Southeast Asia had conveniently adopted these words to define the dialects of Mǐnnán. In those days, the coolies organized them-selves into bāngpài, which were almost always divided by

languages and places of origin, and they ex
darity with their provincial, or prefectural,
arms.

But China's prefectural system has been abolished, its
people forced to adopt a less insular outlook by urbani-
zation and modernization. To define dialects with the
terms "Fujian" and "Chaozhou" is a relic of a bygone age,
and such terms would confuse and be anachronistic if
used today.

Qing Dynasty Administrative Divisions

In the Qing Empire, provinces (shěng) were territorially
divided into prefectures (fǔ), which were in turn divided
into departments (zhóu) and counties (xiàn). Governors
administered provinces, and prefects headed prefectures. Magistrates managed counties, and they possessed both judicial and executive powers.

Departments (zhóu) were usually the capital cities of
prefectures. So, Hangzhou fǔ was a prefecture, and
Hangzhou, its capital.

Strategically important departments were designated
directly administrated departments (zhílizhóu), which
did not govern counties. Such departments were looked
after by magistrates with special knowledge, and these
magistrates were supervised by provincial governors, not
prefectural prefects.

Varieties of Chinese

The EPT test for comparing one language with another is mutual intelligibility. If a speaker of one language variety comprehends a speaker of another variety and vice versa, the two varieties are considered dialects. Otherwise, they are regarded as different languages. Like any early pregnancy test kit, its results are not always correct.

Most linguists consider the many regional Chinese varieties, such as Mandarin, Yuè, or Mǐn, as separate languages because they are mutually unintelligible. (see Fig 2 for details.[28])

Different sub-varieties may even be mutually unintelligible, such as between Northern- and Southern-mǐn, and they are further classified into dialects and subdialects, each named after the region where native speakers live.

The Mandarin languages

The sub-varieties of Mandarin are many. Speakers of northeastern- and southwestern-dialects may find each other incomprehensible. The spoken Mandarin of some key figures in China's history could serve as examples of incomprehensibility. Mao Zedong and Deng Xiaoping spoke two different dialects of the Southwestern Mandarin. Since Zhou Enlai was born in Huai'an, he would have presumably spoken with a dialect of the Jiānghuái Mandarin, but he moved to Tianjin at thirteen. So, his "accent" changed after living among people who speak Jì Lǔ Mandarin.

(Jianghuai refers to the area between Jiangnan and Huainan.)

(Figure 3 classifies the disparate Mandarin languages.[30])

To link the regional variations in spoken Mandarin, the Chinese government promote Pǔtónghuà. Known also as Modern Standard Chinese, it is based largely on the Beijing dialect, but with ér and other characteristically local sounds removed. Distinctive Beijing vocabularies and expressions were also replaced, with elements more commonly found in other varieties of Mandarin.[29]

(Sorry about the hardcore use of Mandarin in this chapter. You may stay with me, or skip to Chapter Three.)

The Yuè languages

Although both Fujian and Guangdong provinces are homes to natives of a few Sinitic languages, each with its own dialects, the Western world commonly labels the Chinese people from these provinces as Fukienese or Cantonese. But such classification is confusing.

Cantonese was derived from "Canton", which in turn was transliterated from the Yuè (Cantonese) pronunciation for Guangdong – "Kwong Dung." At first, the English word referred to Guangdong province, but later it referred to Guangzhou Prefecture or Guangzhou city. The British made no distinction between Canton prefecture and its capital.

Examples of confusion are found in some European accounts of Southeast Asia (especially those of the Portuguese and the Dutch) that regarded the Mǐnnán-speaking Teochew as Cantonese because they are native to Guangdong province.[31]

Even today, Cantonese may mean any one of these categories – Yuè, Yuèhǎi, Guǎngfǔ, or Standard Yuè.

Yuè (Jyut). The term is derived from the kingdom of Nányuè, established in 204 BCE after the Qin Dynasty disintegrated into separate nations. Nányuè comprised parts of the modern Chinese provinces of Guangdong, Guangxi, and Yunnan. And northern Vietnam. The name Vietnam comes from the Vietnamese pronunciation of Nányuè – Nam Việt.

Varieties of the Yuè language – including Yuèhǎi, Luo-Guang, and Sìyì (Sze Yap) – are spoken in the provinces of Guangdong, Guangxi, and the Cantonese diaspora.[32]

Yuèhǎi (Jyut-hoi). Dialects of this language variety include Guǎngfǔ, Zhóngshān, and Sānyì (Sam Yap), and they are spoken by the Yuè people in Guangdong Province, Hong Kong, Macau, and Malaysia.[33]

Guǎngfǔ (Kwong-fu). The name comes from the contraction of the word Guǎngzhóu fǔ, and the language is spoken in the former Guangzhou Prefecture during Manchu rule.[34]

Standard Yuè (Standard Cantonese). It was based on the dialect of the ancient capital of Guangdong Province. But the Xiguan (Sai Kwan) subdialect is near extinction today because outsiders living in that district outnumber the locals. Standard Cantonese is now built around the Guangzhou Pronunciation Dictionary (1983). It is the standard reference for Guangzhou pronunciation, Yuè vocabulary, and Yuè grammar.[35]

As the official language of Guangdong Province, Standard Yuè is the working language for Cantonese programs on Zhujiang TV and CCTV. Still, many natives of Guangdong maintained that designating the Guangzhou dialect as the provincial language is inappropriate because the Yuè language is not the only language spoken in the province.

Some Facts About the "Sanshui (Samsui)" Women

- Not all "Sanshui" Women were from Sanshui County.
- A number were from Siyi (which means four districts) and Qingyuan County.
- All territories were parts of Guangzhou Prefecture.

Their languages and geographical origins (see Fig 4a)[36]

- The female laborers who wore light blue headgears spoke Luoguang Yuè. Largely bounded by uninhabited mountain ranges, Qingyuan was Guangzhou Prefecture's northernmost county.

- Many of those who wore black headgears spoke Taishanese, the most prominent dialect of the Sìyì language.
- It is hard to classify those female laborers who wore red headgears because Sanshui County lies at the borders of Sānyì-, Luoguang-, and Guǎngfǔ-dialect areas.
- The female Hakka laborers, who wore blue headgears, populate all three territories.

Clan wars

Wars were waged out of economic rivalries between different Chinese communities. And in Malaya, it seemed that Chinese migrants were more tolerant of the different language varieties than dialects of the same variety.

Geographical Origins (see Fig 4b)[39]

The "Four Counties"

- Huizhou and Zhaoqing were prefectures. Guangzhou Prefecture was east of Zhaoqing Prefecture and west of Huizhou Prefecture.
- Xinning is known as Taishan (Toisan) today;

Gugang, Xinhui. And both counties were part of Guangzhou Prefecture.

The "Five Counties"

- Panyu. Shunde. Nanhai. Dongguang. Zengcheng.
- All were counties of Guangzhou Prefecture.

The Larut Wars were fought not because the Cantonese recoiled at the sound of the Hakka language, but because of conflict over mining rights and territories.

Panyu. Shunde. Nanhai. Dongguang. Zengcheng. The Hakka people are indigenous to only the last three counties, while the Yuè Chinese inhabited all five counties. All the Yuè members in the Hǎishān Company were Yuèhǎi.[37]

Huizhou. Zhaoqing. Xinning. Gugang. Only Hakka people populated the first prefecture. Both Hakka and Yuè Chinese are natives of the last three territories. All the Yuè members in the Larut Yìxīng Company were *NOT* Yuèhǎi.[38]

Large numbers of coolies dig up ores from tin lodes inside the tropical rainforests of Perak. Their work was segmented to improve efficiency and carried out by different groups of workers, first, miners; second, carpenters, who made formworks and scaffoldings for the mines, as well as building huts, bridges, and water systems for the mining camps; and third, traders, who sup-

plied tools and implements, food and opium to the remote mining camp in return for rights to market tin ore.
And because the Chinese spoke different languages, they
based this division of labor on language to simplify training and encourage cooperation. The separate work is
identified and tabulated below.[40]

Alliances	Hǎishān / Jiàndé	Yìxīng
Deities	Dàbó Gōng	Xuánwǔ
Rulers (Malay)	Ngah Ibrahim	Raja Abdullah
Miners (Hakka)	Zengcheng Hakka	Huizhou Hakka
Carpenters (Yuè)	Yuèhǎi	non-Yuèhǎi
Traders (Mǐnnán)	Hokkien	Teochew

When viewed from the same perspective, the Chinese Funeral Riots of 1846 arose in Singapore, not because the
Teochew, who made up the Yìxīng Company, and the
Straits-Chinese Hokkien, who made up the Jiàndé[41] Society, found each other's Mǐnnán accent grating, but for
power and control over the pepper and gambier plantations. Although cultivating these crops was largely un-
profitable, plantation workers were heavy users of
opium, and the key to securing lucrative revenues was
the control of these opiate-addicted coolies.[42]

The Yìxīng Company in Singapore. Members of the organization were pepper and gambier planters from Riau. These Teochew migrants were shifting cultivators, repeatedly abandoning degraded land and moving into old-growth ("virgin") forests. They later moved to Singapore. Riots broke out in 1846, when the Jiàndé Society appeared and started pepper and gambier planting.[43]

The Jiàndé Society in Singapore. Wealthy Straits-born Chinese with ancestry from Fujian Province dominated the society.

Secret societies were called societies (huì or shè or huìshè), in part because they provided many services for their members. And migrants had so much trouble adjusting to work and life in Malaya.

These societies were secret because they were clamped down tightly. Immediately after the 1867 riots in Penang, the British took the Straits Settlement away from company rule, placing it under the authority of Queen Victoria. That transformed the settlement of the East India Company into an overseas territory of Britain. Penang adopted the laws of England. It got tough with these societies by passing the Suppression of Dangerous Societies Ordinance two years later.[44]

But the laws of England did not apply to Perak at that time. The Hǎishān and Yìxīng Companies were operating in Perak at the behest of Raja Abdullah, who was the son of the former ruler of Perak, and Ngah Ibrahim, who was the administrator of the district of Larut.

(The Raja Muda, or heir apparent, to the former sultan was passed over by the Royal Council in favour of Sultan Ismail, and he later felled out with the Malay headman.)

The Hǎishān, Yìxīng, and Yìfú Companies were called companies (kongsi in Mǐnnán) because each was a business, whose ownership was divided among its shareholders.

Even in the Straits Settlement, comprising Penang, Malacca, and Singapore, it would be more correct to regard the Yìxīng and Yìfú Companies as illicit enterprises for business, or if you prefer, secret companies.

Twenty years after the Suppression of Dangerous Societies Ordinance was legislated, Cecil Clementi Smith replaced it with the Societies Ordinance in 1889. Empowered by the new law, he established the Chinese Advisory Board, whose membership were largely the towkay elite. He stripped the revenue farmers of their "police power" and official status, transferring their influence to the towkays. Towkay, in its literal sense, means "head of a family." It is a Mǐnnán word. And the towkay's business, no doubt, belonged to his family.

At first, all tin merchants were Hakka. Many took loans from the Hokkien merchants in Penang and Malacca, or the Teochew merchants in Penang.[45] The Hokkien and Teochew merchants in turn had credit extended to them by British merchants as "they only needed to put on a clean shirt and turn up at a European godown to receive all they wanted in trade goods."[46]

By the late nineteenth century, Chinese mining companies evolved from a "company structure" to a "tribute system." In this way, the tin merchants reduced their risk, and they were able to hire a much greater number of coolies to search for lodes and dig for ores.[47]

Coolies were given shares of the company in place of wages. If the mine yielded less tin than expected, the merchant loses only the capital cost of the excavation. The coolies were fed, but they worked for nothing.[48]

"Tributes" or payments from profits had to be set aside for, first, the landlord; second, the merchant who provided the finance; and third, the headman, or contractor, of the operations. Ten percent each. The remaining seventy percent would be divided among the coolies. A coolie could own more than one share. He is free to do what he wanted with his share of the proceeds, including hiring new immigrants and paying them from his share.[49]

Accounts were closed after eight months of operations and dividends paid. Tributes had a higher claim to profits than common shares. If the coolies did not get the full seventy percent, the shortfall would be made up when the accounts were closed again in four more months. If the business did not improve at the end of the year, the coolies would not be paid.[50]

These coolies would enter such contracts because many were refugees from China. The Hakka had played a major role in the Taiping Rebellion, which was crushed in 1864 by the Qing government (and their European allies).[51]

But the tin mining industry was nearing sunset. When the sun went below the horizon ...

Both the coolies and their masters could barely make payments to their creditors by the twentieth century. When tin prices fall, many businesses were foreclosed, and some tin merchants became contractors for their creditors.[52]

The Mǐn language

The Mǐn language is named after the Min River, the largest river in Fujian Province. Its tributaries enter the main channel at right angles and crisscross nearly all the northern and central parts of the province. The river and its tributaries are crucial for moving goods, people, and ideas within the mountainous province.

The coastal varieties of the Mǐn language – Southern-mǐn, Pútián-mǐn[53], Eastern-mǐn[54] – were spoken by nearly all Mǐn migrants to Southeast Asia, including the British colony of Singapore.

The Southern-mǐn language (see Fig 5)

Although the southern part of Fujian Province is not served by the Min river system, its people are known as Southern-mǐn or Mǐnnán (Bân-lâm). Mǐnnán dialects are named after four prefectures in the Qing Empire.

- Chaozhou (Guangdong Province)
- Quanzhou (Fujian Province)
- Zhangzhou (Fujian Province)
- Taiwan-Xiamen Defense Region (Fujian Province) (The Xiamen dialect is also known as the Taiwanese language.)

These dialects spread over two provinces. Mǐnnán migrants to Southeast Asia were natives of either "Chaozhou" (Teochew) or "Fujian" (Hokkien). But Fujian

Province, unlike Guangdong, has no provincial language, its official language being Pǔtónghuà. To make themselves clear, the "Hokkien" on both sides of the Taiwan Strait (Fujian Province, China; and Taiwan) consider themselves to be Fúlǎo (Hoklo)[55].

Quánzhóu (Chinchew) dialect[56]

The port of Quanzhou was the busiest in China, and its strong growth increased the kingdom's volume of maritime foreign trade. During the Song dynasty, maritime foreign trade exceeded the amount of overland foreign trade for the first time in history. Continued growth of the port during the Yuan era led Marco Polo to visit it, and he described it as one of the greatest port in the world, comparing it to Alexandria of Egypt. The city was also known as Zaytoun, the Arabic word for olive. The olive tree is a symbol of prosperity in the Middle East, and the olive branch, the symbol for peace.

Many Quanzhou traders settled in the kingdoms of Malacca, Srivijaya, Majapahit, and Tondo.

From their homes in the kingdom of Tondo, Luzon traders sailed across Southeast Asia, selling Chinese goods, and they were considered "Chinese" by the people they met. Tondo is known as Manila today.

Even when the Ming dynasty banned maritime activities, during prohibitions that were in place between 1368 and 1567, Admiral Zheng-he used Quanzhou as the staging base and supply depot for his expeditions.

In nineteenth-century Singapore, the Quanzhou Chinese were entrepôt traders, sailing from port to port, buying produce that Quanzhou middlemen in the Malay Archipelago secured from indigenous producers and selling their cargoes to the European agency houses in the colony. They were so prevalent in these activities that the word "chinchew" became a synonym for supercargo.

A supercargo is the ship-owner's representative on board a merchant vessel. He is in charge of the cargo. So he manages the trade, selling the merchandise at ports where the vessel sails and buying goods for the return voyage.

Subdialects of Quanzhou include Nan'an (Lam Ann), Jinjiang (Chin Kang), Anxi, and Hui'an.

Yǒngchūn (Eng Choon) subdialect

The Yongzheng Emperor, successor to the Kangxi Emperor and father of the Qianlong Emperor, removed Yongchun County from Quanzhou Prefecture in 1734, upgrading it into a directly administered department, Yǒngchūn Zhílìzhóu.

As tigers roamed among entangled trees in the forest-covered land of Yongchun, life was hard for everyone. Many left the rugged interior of Fujian Province for Southeast Asia. In Malaysia, where they were largely small acreage farm owners who worked on their own land, they represented the largest number of Fúlǎo (Hoklo).

Some consider Yǒngchūn a dialect of Mǐnnán. Others consider it a subdialect of Quanzhou.

Zhāngzhóu (Changchew) dialect[57]

The two major cities of Zhangzhou Prefecture were Changtai and Moon Harbor (Yuegang).

During the Ming dynasty, the former was the prefectural capital, and the latter was a haven for smugglers when maritime trade was forbidden. After the Ming dynasty loosened its ban on maritime trade in 1567, Moon Harbor became China's only overseas trading port.

After the Manchus conquered China, the great consolidator of the Qing Empire fought Ming loyalists based in Taiwan. From his throne in the Forbidden City, the Kangxi Emperor, who was fourth in the line of rulers from his family and the first to be born on Chinese soil, decreed coastal areas to be evacuated in 1661. The Great Clearance (yánhǎi qiānjiè) was a measure to deny support and supplies to the anti-Qing movement. The emperor did not rescind his orders until 1669, and it laid waste Moon Harbor.

The trading port was later renamed Haicheng.

Many Chinese from Zhangzhou settled in British Penang, the Sultanate of Deli (present day Medan), Thanlyin (present day Yangon), Saigon, Spanish East Indies, Jung Ceylon (present day Phuket), and Portuguese Malacca.

In Penang, they traded rubber and tin during British rule, prospering with the economic expansion of Kedah, Perak, and Province Wellesley. They flourished even more by trading tobacco.[58] The Zhangzhou Chinese in Penang and Medan profited from the spectacular growth of large-scale plantations at the Dutch residency in the East Coast of Sumatra.

(Medan was the main town of the Dutch residency, where the guilder was legal tender. But foreign currencies were used in nearly all monetary transactions.)

In Singapore, some of them were opium revenue farmers. The Haicheng bāng comprised Malaccan Chinese of Haicheng ancestry. Their social activities revolved around Tiān-Fǔ-Góng (Thian Hock Keng) Temple.[59] Built in 1839, the temple is consecrated to Māzǔ, evincing their seafaring heritage.

The rival Changtai bāng was also named after their subdialect. It comprised Penang Chinese of Changtai ancestry. They centered their social lives on the Changtai Guild Hall and the Qīng-yuán-zhēn-jūn Temple[60], where they worshiped Dàbó Gōng. Both the guild hall and the temple were founded in 1949, some three years after the Jiàndé Huì[61] appeared in Singapore.

The Sultanate of Johor

The Johor Empire (see Fig 1 for locator map) was partitioned into two puppet states when Singapore was established as a colony in 1819. The Johor Sultanate (in blue) was the puppet of the British; the Riau-Lingga Sultanate (in red), Dutch.

The Johor Sultanate comprised the kingdom of Pahang, and the kingdom of Johor and Singapore. Pahang was held by the bendahara. Johor and Singapore were held by the temenggung.

(Bendaharas and temenggungs were hereditary titles, given to important officials appointed by the sultan.)

Cháoshàn (Teoswa) dialect[62]

After the 1854 Hokkien-Teochew riots in Singapore, many Chaozhou (Mǐnnán: Teochew) Chinese moved to Johor, where they found a congenial home with the temenggung. The temenggung later declared himself the Maharaja of Johor, an independent ruler. And these Chaozhou Chinese, who were members of the Yìxīng Company, transformed themselves into revenue farmers in the sovereign state.

Another group of Chaozhou opium revenue farmers operated in Singapore. The Tan Clan (Mǐnnán: Seh Tan) worshiped at the Yuè-hǎi-qīng Temple (Wak Hai Cheng Bio). Its clansmen were Chinese with ancestry from Chenghai District, Chaozhou Prefecture.

The Kangxi Emperor permitted the port in Chenghai District to import rice from Siam in 1722. This main Chinese port was well known beyond China's borders, appearing on a map published in Britain in 1875. As many as one-and-a-half million people left the port for Siam, over the hundred-year rule of the four emperors: Qianlong, Jiaqing, Daoguang, and Xianfeng.

Today, the seaport is known as the Old Port of Zhanglin (Zhānglín Gǔgǎng).

Another port, Shantou, was carved out of Chenghai District and opened for foreign trade after the Second Opium War. But the Chinese continued to use the "Old Port" because it was the Europeans who set up Shantou's docks, warehouses, and other port facilities.

Out of the eight "Poit-ip" districts of Chaozhou Prefecture, where Mǐnnán was (and is still) spoken, three were powerful administrative centers – Haiyang, Chaoyang, Jieyang.

- *Haiyang* was the capital of Chaozhou Prefecture in the Qing Empire.
- *Chaoyang* was directly overseen by the General Supervisory and Military Command in the Qing Empire.
- *Jieyang* was the administrative center for the area covering today's Chaoshan, Longyan, and Zhangzhou during the Han dynasty.

Their names, which coincidentally contained the character "yang", were used to define the subdialects of Chaozhou.

But the Nationalist government abolished the prefectural system, so Chaozhou Prefecture does not exist today. Also, the communist government placed the two Hakka-speaking districts under Meizhou city in 1988.

Today, Nan'ao Island is added to the original "eight districts." Haiyang is renamed Chao'an and divided into two districts. Chenghai is also divided into two districts. Chaoyang and Jieyang are each divided into three districts, making up fifteen Mĭnnán-speaking districts. Today, these fifteen are part of three cities: Chaozhou, Shantou, and Jieyang. And the three cities make up a single metropolitan area, Chaoshan, with its administrative center in Shantou.

In place of the three "yang", Chaozhou, Shantou, and Jieyang are used today to define the subdialects of Chaoshan, which in turn is a dialect of Mĭnnán. Just in case you haven't noticed, Chaoshan is a word made by shortening and combining "Chaozhou" and "Shantou."

During the nineteenth-century, the Chaoshan Chinese in Singapore bartered British manufactures for rice and other foodstuff. Their trading partners were the Chaoshan Chinese in Bangkok and Sóc Trăng, a province in the Mekong Delta of southern Vietnam.

The Zhangzhou Chinese set up a bilateral trade between Saigon and Singapore, but they were later forced out of business by the French tariff on Singapore's exports. Later, to support the French economy, the colonial ruler converted agricultural farmlands around Saigon into tea, coffee, and rubber plantations.

The three monuments to the Maritime Silk Road are first, Quanzhou, port of the Southern Song Dynasty; then, Yuegang, port of the Ming; and after that, Zhanglin, port of the mid-Qing.[63] And, as you may have noticed by now, all three are in Mǐnnán-speaking communities. Two other ports, however, were more important for shipping the Mǐnnán language to Singapore. Both Xiamen and Jinmen are in territories where people speak the ...

Xiàmén (Amoy) dialect

Xiamen prospered after the Kangxi Emperor placed it under the Taiwan-Xiamen Defense Region in 1684 and gave it the privilege of foreign trade. Its traders sailed to the Javanese side of the Sundra Straits, where they sold tea to Dutchmen and Englishmen at the markets of Banten. During the seventeenth and eighteenth century, it was the principal Chinese port that traded with the South Seas (Nanyang), so Xiamen was the origin of most Chinese migrants to Southeast Asia.

Its fortune waned after the Qianlong emperor established the Canton System in 1757, letting the British East India Company trade on Chinese soil. The policy restricted maritime trade to Guangzhou, and it gave monopoly trading rights to private Chinese merchants.

At Banten, the Europeans had exchanged silver for tea. At Guangzhou, the EIC improved their compensation, first, by supplementing taxes for the emperor; second, by helping the hong merchants maximize profits without ship construction or sea carriage; and third, by meeting the need for convenience of the Yuè Chinese. The EIC took the opium trade into their neighborhood.

The Canton System later broke down, triggering the First Opium War in 1839. After the war, the EIC forced the emperor to give away the ports of Guangzhou and Xiamen, among others, as concessions. While the taipans and hong merchants extended their business to Shanghai and other British enclaves, the Xiamen merchants shifted into Jinmen (Quemoy).

The "Golden Gate" island served as a sanctuary from the exactions of Chinese emperors and the exploitations of various East India Companies.

Subdialects of the Xiamen dialect include Tong'an (Tung Ann) and Jinmen.

- Tong'an people represented the third largest number of Fúlăo in Malaysia.
- Jinmen Islands is a part of the *Republic of China (ROC)* today, and Taipei uses the Mĭnnán pronunciation for its English name: *Kinmen County of Fujian Province.*

Pútián-mĭn

The emperors of the Song dynasty stationed the Xinghua (Henghua) Army at Putian and Xianyou counties, ceding these two counties from Quanzhou prefecture and placing them under the military command. The army remained for hundreds of years until the Qing dynasty closed the garrison.[64]

As a garrison community, and for such a long time, the civilian population speaks Púxiān huà, a hybrid language of the Quanzhou dialect and the military language. Xianyou County is today merged into Putian, and the Púxiān language is also known as Pútián language.

Eastern-mǐn

Fuqing (Hokchia) is a subdialect of Fuzhou (Hokchew). And Fuzhou, Fu'an, and Manjiang are dialects of Eastern-mǐn, also known as the Mǐn Dóng language.

During the late nineteenth and early twentieth century, Pútián and Eastern-mǐn immigrants in Singapore usually found work as rickshaw pullers, vocations that were reasonably well-paid, considering that, in 1867, oversight of the coolie town was merely transferred from the evil-inhalant company, which was based in Bengal, to the circumlocution office, which was based in London.

In 1908, an experienced puller earned between $1.70 and $2.00 a day. That's more than the daily wage of an ordinary coolie, 50 cents; a laborer at the tin mines, 70 cents; and a coal coolie, not more than $1.00[65] – each one earning more than Ah-Q[66] in China.

Rickshawmen divided Singapore into territorial monopolies. They kept to tightly defined areas, huddling together for company and protection by secret societies of their own community.[67]

The Fúzhóu and Fúqīng plied their trade at the Queen Street and Johore Road district. Fúqīng pullers also controlled Raffles Hotel, River Valley Road, and Tank Road Railway Station.[68]

The Pútián claimed the length of Orchard Road and areas around Europe Hotel their territory.[69] They were truly an army heritage. In 1919, they militantly confronted City Hall, calling for rickshaw fares to be doubled.[70] Many were also engaged in rickshaw repairs[71], which might not be so different from gun-carriage repairs.

The Fúlǎo's turf lay around Beach Road Market and Telok Ayer Basin.[72] Many were from Hui'an County, Quanzhou Prefecture.[73]

Sitiawan, a town in Perak, and the areas surrounding it were home to descendants of immigrants who spoke in the Eastern-mǐn language. A choir boy at the town grew up to fight for the Malayan People's Anti-Japanese Army during the Second World War. He was the liaison officer between the Chinese resistance and the British military in Southeast Asia. To the British, he was known by his Mandarin name, "Cheng [sic Chen] Ping."

A few years after the war, he became "Public Enemy No. 1", making it to the front page of the Straits Times in 1951. As reported by the Singapore newspaper, he was a wanted man with a reward of $250,000 for information leading to his capture. Underneath the headline was a large mug shot, captioned "THIS IS CHIN PENG ...", and from there the Hakka name stuck.[74]

For years afterward, the Hak people (or Hakka) in Singapore carried identity cards that classified their dialect as Khek, a Mǐnnán word. (It's tempting to infer a cause-and-effect connection, but that's getting too cosmological.)

The term "Hakka" is unambiguous, but since Mǐnnán words have been replaced with Mandarin for the rest of this publication –

Hokkien is replaced with Fúlǎo;

Teochew, Cháoshàn;

both Hokkien and Teochew, Mǐnnán;

Hokchew, Fúzhóu;

Hokchia, Fúqīng;

both Hokchew and Hokchia, Eastern-mǐn;

Henghwa, Pútián;

Cantonese, Yuè or Yuèhǎi

– I might as well replace Hakka with Kèjiā.

And, for the record, I'm an equal-opportunity crack-pot.

Of gods and men and their associations in Singapore

The Fujian guild hall. It was founded inside the Tiān-fǔ-gōng Temple in 1840. The temple lost its waterfront after reclamation, and the guild hall moved to its own premises, built on new land created from the sea.

At first, the guild hall admitted only the Fúlǎo into the association. After more than a hundred years, during the nineteen-fifties, it started offering membership to all from Fujian Province[75], such as Eastern-mǐn-speakers from Fuzhou or Kèjiā-speakers from Longyan.

The Cháoshàn foundation. It was also founded inside a temple. One side of the Yuè-hǎi-qīng Temple was dedicated to Māzǔ goddess, the red-robed patron of the seas, and the other side was for their ancestors.

Other Cháoshàn Chinese. Those who were members of the Yìxīng Company worshiped Xuánwǔ[76], the patron deity of the Ming emperors. After the Chinese Funeral Riots of 1846, a significant part of the company moved to Johor, where they built the Johor Bahru Old Chinese Temple and worship the "Dark Warrior."

Many members of the company had refused to take part in temple ceremonies or give tithes to the company because they converted to Catholicism. Rumors of converts having illicit opium in their plantations abound, adding fuel to the fire. Opium smuggling violated the monopoly of the company, and a five-day massacre in 1851 was the reprisal. The Anti-Catholics Riot left about thirty gambier farms razed.

The Hǎishān Company and the Jiàndé Society. Members of both organizations were devotees of Dàbó Gōng (Tuapek Kong). The bearded "Grand Uncle" is the patron of urban businessmen, and he is said to set foot on Penang forty years before Francis Light.

The Fúdé Temple (Fuk Tak Chi) in Singapore was devoted to Dàbó Gōng. But it was the Yuè and Kèjiā Chinese who built this temple in 1824. That was five years after Stamford Raffles started to welcome immigrants to his new trading outpost. The devotees at the temple were apparently not construction workers because building tradesmen worshiped Lǔ Bān (Lo Pan)[77]. Were they migrants from Penang? Were they recruiters for the Hǎishān Company and its Yuè branch, Guǎng Hǎishān (Kwong Hai San)?

The Changtai bāng were also worshippers of Dàbó Gōng. The leader[78] of the bāng paid for repair and improvement work at Fúdé Temple in 1869. But neither the Qīng-yuán-zhēn-jūn Temple nor the Changtai Guild Hall remains in Singapore today.

The Héhé Society. Its members were devotees of Lǔ Bān. The "second faction chief" founded a Lǔ Bān temple in Kamunting after he signed the Treaty of Pangkor.

The Yǒngchūn Chinese. A lot of them were worshippers of Fǎ Zhǔgōng (Huat Chu Kong), meaning "Master of the Way." The legendary mystic warrior was a master of Daoism and Dào martial arts. After assisting people in the many villages throughout the land with his myriad exploits and deeds, he ascended into deityhood. The black-face deity is the guardian of villages, protecting farmers from plagues.

The Pútián Chinese. They were devotees of Māzǔ and the Sanyi religion. The latter combines elements of Confucian, Daoism, and Buddhism. Both the sea goddess and the founder of the "Three in the One" religion were born in Putian County.

The Methodist movement. The oldest Chinese-speaking Methodist church in Singapore was founded in 1889. Its founder preached in Malay, and an interpreter translated his sermons into Fúlǎo, reaching out to the immigrant Chinese. Among those who gathered to hear Dr Benjamin Franklin West were opium addicts.

By the mid-eighteen-nineties, Telok Ayer Chinese Methodist Church had 170 members. Linguistic diversity also increased as Pútián, Fúqīng, and Fúzhōu members were added to their number.

After its founder returned to America, Dr Heinrich Ludwig Emil Luering, who was conversant in both Mǐnnán and Eastern-mǐn, headed the church. Luering recruited a pastor from Fuzhou to look after the Eastern-mǐn-speaking congregation, which soon formed the majority. He hired another pastor to keep the Mǐnnán congregation.[79]

The Yuè women. Those working as nannies, housekeepers, or babysitters were devotees of Lady Jīnhuā (Kam Fa), who is assisted by twelve "wet-nurses." These twelve deities protect babies, from birth until they reach their teens. The Golden Flower Shrine, for the mother goddess and her attendant deities, was at first located near the crossroad where Albert Street and Queen Street meet. But when the neighborhood was redeveloped in 1978, the temple had to move to a private house at Mountbatten Road.

I am making the exposé below, albeit risking accusations of being a dao-jiang-hu, which in Shanghainèse means "one who is full of crap."

By the end of the nineteenth-century, migrants in Singapore included those from two cities built on river confluxes – Ningpo and Wenzhou.[80] Ningpo's original settlement began where three rivers converge, and the Y-shaped Sanjiang Kou is now a famous downtown landmark.

Wenzhou was established on a T-shaped confluence. And in that "mild and pleasant" city today, a township, a port and a marina, many government institutions, and commercial organizations are given the name Sanjiang, which means river confluence.

Ningpo and Wenzhou languages are dialects of the Wú language. Its various dialects are mutually intelligible to some extent.

Wú Chinese, for instance, enjoy three main types of operas, Kūnqǔ, Yuèjù, and Huájīxì. The first is an opera sung in a Suzhou subdialect (Kunshan). The second, a musical theater performed with a dialect spoken in Zhejiang (Shaoxing). The third, a farce in the Shanghainese dialect.

Wenzhou dialect is an outlier. Because it is so divergent, the other Wú people commonly believed that during the Sino-Japanese and Sino-Vietnamese wars, Wenzhou people were enlisted as code talkers, using their dialect as a means of secret communication.

Wú Chinese are usually known as Jiāngzhè people, named after the abbreviations for Jiangsu and Zhejiang in the late Qing Empire; or Jiāngnán people, named after a province in the early Qing Empire; or even Wúyuè people, named after the Wúyuè kingdom during the Five Dynasties and Ten Kingdoms period, a time of political disturbance from 907 to 979.[81] But in Singapore, the term used was "Sanjiang" (Sam Kiang).

"Sanjiang" is used in the Tribute of Yu, one of the Five Classics of ancient Chinese literature, to denote the three rivers – Yellow, Huai, and Yangtze. Because of silting and heavy floods, the Yellow River sometimes changed its course, running southward into the Huai River. Water from the Huai River pooled up in Lake Hongze and then drained into the Yangtze. Sometimes river sediment choked up the Yangtze and water backed up into Lake Hongze. A mythical leader in the book, Yu the Great, contained the floods of these rivers with his body. Today, with more progress but less success, the government in China control floods with a system of dams, levees, dredging operations ... and a plan to evacuate communities when the system fail.

Alluding to the Golden Triangle of the Yangtze from which the Wú-speakers emigrated, this fifth-century BCE term would never go out of style. The word "Sanjiang" exuded refinement because cultural authenticity, from the perspective of Chinese tradition, is more discernible with age.

In the past, Singaporeans used the term "Shanghainese" interchangeably with "Sanjiang Chinese", probably because that language was the common language among speakers of the different Wú dialects[82], or probably because Shanghainese was the label British immigration officials used for all who embarked from Shanghai for Malaya[83], or even because, if disbelief were to be suspended for a moment, notorious Shanghainese gangsters raised the anxiety of combat-hardened veterans in Singapore's secret societies.

But because the Shanghainese label improved the fortunes for many Sanjiang businesses, such as furniture or piano companies, they continued to assume the label. Shanghainese carpentry was known for its quality and was sought after by hotels, Europeans, and wealthy Chinese families in Singapore. Many supposedly Shanghainese-owned businesses were started by Wenzhou and Ningbo Chinese.[84]

Many Sanjiang association elders habitually used the terms "Sanjiang" and "Shanghainese" synonymously. So, the community was known as the Shanghai bāng.[85]

When the Sanjiang association was founded in 1906, the association redefined "Sanjiang" to mean the three provinces: Jiangsu, Zhejiang, and Jiangxi.[86] Zhejiang has four spoken languages; Jiangsu, three; and Jiangxi, three. Nevertheless, all migrants from the three provinces were considered Shanghainese.[87]

The languages spoken in:
- *Zhejiang* are Wú, Mǐn, Gàn, Jiānghuái Mandarin.
- *Jiangsu* are Wú, Jiānghuái Mandarin, Zhóngyuán Mandarin.
- *Jiangxi* are Gàn, Kèjiā, Jiānghuái Mandarin.

Yet again, the association broadened, in its constitution in 1945, the term "Sanjiang" to include immigrants from provinces along the Yangtze River, Yellow River, and Amur River (Heilong Jiang).[88] From river mouths to upland sources, around meanders and between tributaries, the association now draws its members from half of China (as well as parts of Russia and Mongolia).

And so, dear reader, don't ever go up against the San-jiang association in a game of wéiqí.

Chapter 3

• • • • • • • • • •

COLONIAL SCHOOLS
An Imperial education system

Decapitation awaited those returning to China after going abroad, since emigration was forbidden in the Empire of the Great Qing. So most early Chinese migrants to Singapore were those born in the Malay Archipelago, especially Malacca and Penang, where their families had lived for generations.

In 1821, with only 1,150 on the island, the Chinese formed nearly twenty percent of the population.[89] By 1830, their number increased to 6,555, making up almost forty percent of those living in the British settlement.[90] After the First Opium War, the Manchu government permitted indentured laborers to migrate, and the Chinese soon became the greater part of Singapore's population. But their children were not the majority of youth on the island, since most coolies neither settled nor raised families in the colony.

Reverend Thomsen reported one Yuè school with twelve boys at Kampong Glam, and another with eight boys at Pekin Street in 1829. (Could the Yuè school at Pekin Street be housed inside the Fúdé Temple?) He also reported a Fúlǎo school with twenty-two boys at Pekin Street, and an English school with forty-eight boys. The school hired one English master and three native (Malay) masters. English students paid $15, natives $4, and for extra subjects $10.[91]

Girls were not reported to be attending school at that time. Perhaps it was believed that they could only get married or get an education. Not both. And sending them to school would have consigned them to spinsterhood, a sentiment shared by both Asian and European families.

The English-medium Schools

Raffles Institution started to admit pupils only from 1837, although it was founded in 1823. Then named the Singapore Institution, its trustees ran out of donor money halfway through the build and abandoned it. Twelve years later, the East India Company revived the school, and after two more years, they finished the restoration. Still, the school offered education to only the sons of EIC employees and the children of Malay royalty.[92]

Raffles Girls' School (RGS) was opened at Raffles Institution in 1844, with six boarders and five day-scholars. To make room at the boys' school for seventeen boy pupils who were sent by the King of Siam, the girls' school moved into a house on the opposite side of Bras Basah Road in 1871. Ten years later, construction started for a new building on the land behind the boys' school. The construction finished in 1883, and RGS moved into its own premises that year.[93]

Saint Joseph's Institution was founded in 1852 as Saint John's Institution, using a former chapel as the school premises. Within a year, a hut with thatched roof had to be erected to accommodate the overflow from the converted chapel.[94] Its first students were probably Kristang, a people of mixed Portuguese and Malaccan descent.

St Andrew's School started as a small private school founded by two Chinese Anglicans in the eighteen-fifties. A few years later, St Andrew's Church started an organization for missions, recruiting Reverend Edward Sherman Venn, who adopted the school in 1862 to further its work.[95] The missionary organization renamed Sim Quee's School as the St Andrew's Church of England Mission School, funding it and retaining its two Chinese owners as headmasters. It was unusual for Asians to head missionary schools at that time.[96]

The British transferred the colony from the East India Company to the Colonial Office in 1867. The Straits Settlements became a separate Crown colony, but its education policy remained unchanged.

Cheang Wan Seng School was founded by the leader[97] of the Changtai bāng in 1875. He named it after his business, whose "chop name" [98] was Wan Seng.[99] The founder paid all expenses and provided free education for the poor, accepting pupils of all ages and religion. The daily attendance was ninety students by its second year of operation. Later, the school was moved to Havelock Road and renamed after the eldest son[100] of the founder. After his son passed away in 1901, the school was shuttered, leaving 216 students to find new schools for themselves.[101]

St. Anthony's School was established in 1879 by the Catholic Portuguese Mission of Singapore. It was then called St. Anna's School and admitted both boys and girls. The six pupils of the first enrollment enjoyed free tuition.[102]

Secondary Schools. In 1884, Raffles Institution started post-primary classes.

The Bilingual Schools

Anglo-Chinese Free School was set up in 1885 by Gan Eng-seng. The school offered free education to the children of the poor. Three years later, it became an aided school, gaining both government recognition and grants. It taught in both English and Fúlǎo[103], and its bilingual program was a formula for success. The school enrolled a record 167 students in 1890, and its enrollment rose to an all-time high of ninety-four percent in 1892. After the founder passed away in 1899, it stopped teaching in Chinese, and fees were introduced because of financial difficulties. In 1923, the school was renamed after its founder (GESS).[104]

Anglo-Chinese School (ACS) was founded by William Fitz-james Oldham in 1886. The bishop of the Methodist Mission saw young boys wandering aimlessly in the streets, and he started the school as an extension ministry of the Methodist Church. ACS is not connected in any way with the school founded by Gan the year before. It was named Anglo-Chinese School because lessons were conducted in English at night and in Chinese (probably Fúlǎo) during the afternoon. ACS admitted 13 pupils in its first year, and it increased its enrollment to 104 the following year.[105]

Singapore Chinese Girls' School was founded in 1899. It was the first all-girls Peranakan school, with an English headmistress and seven girls on the register.[106] The school taught Romanized Malay, Chinese (maybe Baba Hokkien), Arithmetic, Geography, Music, and Sewing to equip young girls for their future roles as (Nyonya) wives and mothers.[107]

The Malay-medium Schools

Kampong Glam Malay Branch School was founded with twelve Malay boys in 1876. Students who finished primary school in the Malay classes were sent to the Malay College at Telok Blangah.

The Malay "college" was closed in 1882. Raffles Institution revived Malay classes in 1885, but abandoned that after eight years for lack of support.

The school at Kampong Glam became a feeder school for Raffles Institution. In 1897, the school formed its first soccer team. Each year, many of its talented soccer players went on to play in the senior ranks for Raffles' soccer team. The school was later renamed Victoria School, becoming the second government secondary school in Singapore.[108]

The Feeder School System

Toward the end of the nineteenth century, the government gave grants-in-aid to private English-medium schools, in return for control over their activities. After the turn of the century, these aided schools were taken over for direct management.

After the feeder system was set up in 1903, Raffles Institution discontinued its primary classes and focused entirely on secondary education. It admitted students from the aided schools, preparing them for the "Junior Cambridge" and "Senior Cambridge" examinations. Passing these examinations might have secured school leavers places at Raffles College, but they had to wait until 1928 to enroll. Or they could further their studies abroad without delay.

During the nineteen-tens, Anglo-Chinese School (Methodism), Saint Joseph's Institution (Catholicism), and Saint Andrew's School (Anglicanism) ceased to be feeder schools for Raffles Institution after they started their own classes for the Junior and Senior Cambridge examinations.

Locked in by rivalry, the three aided secondary schools gave places only to students from their feeder schools, which were primary schools founded by parochial churches. It was preposterous, at that time, for Saint Andrew's School to feed a hungry young mind from a Catholic primary school, or for Saint Joseph's Institution to help a nerdy child from a Methodist primary school. As expected, Anglo-Chinese School reciprocated these favors by inviting no Catholic or Anglican pupil to its pedagogical table.

As late as 1919, the government gave financial help to only one Chinese school for boys, with an average enrollment of seventeen, and one Chinese school for girls, with an average enrollment of forty-nine.[109] It was not until 1947 that Chinese schools were included in the rigid feeding pattern.[110]

The Chinese-medium Schools

St Margaret's School was founded in Singapore as Chinese Girls' School in 1842 by Mrs Maria Dyer. She speaks the Fúlǎo dialect, and she had previously handed over more than four Fúlǎo schools in Penang. The Penang schools had a total of seventy-nine pupils.[111] The Singapore school was started with the approval of the London Missionary Society, and it operated out of a shophouse along North Bridge Road.

(Commonly seen in urban Southeast Asia, shophouses are two or three stories high with a shop on the ground floor and a residence above. The buildings are erected next to each other, forming a line. A row of shophouses usually spans the full extent permitted by zoning and building ordinances.)

To run the shopschool, funds were partly raised from the closure of the Chinese mission in Penang and the contributions of Samuel Garling, the Resident Councilor of Penang. Mrs Dyers took in girls who were orphans and had fallen victims of child slavery (mui tsai). The primary school is now along Wilkie Road, its affiliated secondary school along Farrer Road. It has been renamed in honor of Queen Margaret of Scotland.

Chóngwén Gé was built next to Tiān-fǔ-gōng Temple in 1849. The lower floor was used for teaching and the upper floor consecrated to Wénchāng Dìjūn. The pavilion for the God of Culture and Literature was sponsored by the leaders of the Fúlǎo and the Cháoshàn community.[112]

Cuì-yīng (Chui Eng) Chinese School was founded in 1854 by the leader of the Fúlǎo community. It was the largest Chinese school at that time.[113] Its name alluded to a gathering of talent from the British dominions, scoffing the English schools – one that admitted only children of nobility and the other that won't admit children of Pagans. After a hundred years of teaching, the school closed its doors for the last time, in 1954.

Chongfu School. After the boys were moved from Chóngwén Gé to Cuì-yīng, the vacated space was used to found Chong Hock Girls' School. The school has since moved out of Chóngwén Gé, become co-educational, and used the Mandarin pronunciation for its English name.

The British and the French forced the Qing government to open many more treaty ports after the Second Opium War. Foreign legations could operate even in the capital, Beijing. Since the Chinese government was unable to enforce its restrictions on emigration, it was possible to return to their ancestral homes in China and study there. Nevertheless, the Cháoshàn were more likely than the Fúlǎo to send their children to China for education, as the latter were satisfied with education in the Straits Settlement.[114] The former were also more likely to become Roman Catholics.

Holy Innocents' Boys School was the first Chinese mission school. It was founded as Tao Nan School in 1892 by the Church of the Nativity of the Blessed Virgin Mary. The school taught in the language of Chinese farmers at Serangoon district – Cháoshàn. In 1920, the school was renamed.[115]

Apart from Reverend Thomsen's account, no other record is found of education given in the languages of the non-Mǐnnán Chinese by schools in nineteenth-century Singapore.

Using Mandarin

During the Ming and Qing dynasty, Mandarin was known as Guānhuà, which means "the language of the officials." After the nationalists established the Republic of China in 1912, they replaced it with Guóyǔ, which means "national language." They hoped the newly coined term would encourage the Chinese people, who are from disparate language groups, to adopt the national language and foster a pan-China identity.

In British Malaya, however, the movement was unsuccessful at first because there was no practical use for Mandarin.

The Qing government founded Jinan Academy at Nanjing in 1907. It was the first middle school to admit students from overseas primary schools. But it was closed at the outbreak of the Xinhai Revolution in 1911. After the revolution, Yuan Shikai, the autocratic president of the new republic, refused to reopen the academy in Nanjing.

That spurred Tan Kah-kee, a philanthropist, to set up Chinese High School in Singapore.

After the Guomindang nationalists secured their capital at Nanjing in 1927, they relocated Jinan Academy to Shanghai. The school was reopened as Jinan National University, and it admitted students from overseas high schools, including those from Singapore.[116]

Mandarin became essential for higher education in China.

Political awakening of the Chinese

During China's struggle against Japan over conflicting interests in Korea, the emperor whose reign was influenced by the empress mother appealed to the Nanyang Chinese for financial support, and he formally abrogated the emigration prohibition in 1893.

The conflict led to the First Sino-Japanese War, 1894–1895. After the Guangxu Emperor was defeated by the Meiji Emperor, foreign powers scrambled for concessions, and they partitioned China into spheres of influence.

Dissatisfied with the plight of their country, two Chinese intellectuals were divided in their responses to the Guangxu Emperor and the Empress Dowager Cixi.

- Sun Yat-sen tried to start a revolution in Guangzhou, but the First Guangzhou Uprising failed.
- Kang Youwei persuaded the emperor to introduce a series of radical reforms, such as establishing a constitutional monarchy, but the Empress Dowager and her entourage of conservative officials crushed the Hundred Days' Reform.

Both took refuge by globetrotting abroad, each independently from the other. During their many visits to Singapore, they solicited support from the Chinese community, and they recommended changes that sparked a revival of Chinese education in the British colony.

At the same time, the emperor made his overture. He adhered to the Confucian concept of political meritocracy and opened China's education system for the overseas Chinese. That gave them prospects for upward mobility.

The Chinese community in Singapore responded to these proposals and set up "modern" schools. But because these Confucianism school were run by sectarian groups, they taught in different Sinitic languages. In 1905, the Kèjiā started the first modern school, Yingxin (Yin Sin) School. The next year, they started another, Qifa (Khee Fatt) School; in the same year, the Cháoshàn set up Duanmeng (Tuan Mong) School, and the Yuè established Yangzheng (Yeung Ching) School. In 1910, the Hainanese set up Yuying (Yoke Eng) School.[117]

The Anglo-Chinese Free School (GESS) also followed the trend. In 1913, it resumed teaching a second language and made the subject compulsory.[118]

The Fúlǎo set up their first modern school in 1906.[119] Three years later, Toh Lam School started to admit pupils from other dialect groups, the first Chinese school to do so.[120] In 1916, it began to teach in Mandarin, also the first school to do so.[121] Years later, the school based its English name on Mandarin instead of Fúlǎo. But Tao Nan is the romanized spelling based on the Wade-Giles system, which the school uses to this day.

Schools for girls were established in Singapore after the Qing dynasty was overthrown in China – Zhonghua in 1911, Nanyang in 1917, and Nanhua also in 1917. This overturned 2,500 years of oppressive[122] Confucian ideology. When the Qing reformer Kang promoted Confucianism, it was an antidote against "moral degeneration" and indiscriminate Westernization. But the New Culture Movement[123] of the nineteen-tens and nineteen-twenties called for a new Chinese culture to be created, with values based on global and western standards, including women's liberation.

In 1920, the Pútián Chinese started their modern school, Hong Wen School. It used the Mandarin pronunciation for its English name.

Schools also started night sessions for children who worked during the day. (Even as late as 1954, the government did not object to child labor.[124])

The plea for the community to do something for adult illiteracy was incessant, especially among the Hainanese. Night schools were also established in reading rooms. That provided study opportunities for adults. By 1919, the Hainanese community had four night schools[125].

Political apathy

A Chinese Christian missionary founded the first reading room in 1903. The Xīngzhóu (Sin Chew) Reading Room provided reading materials for the poor Chinese in Singapore, and it gave him opportunities to evangelize.

In 1911, the Cháoshàn community founded Tóngdé (Tung Teh) Reading Room. In 1912, the Kèjiā founded Zhìtóng (Chih Tung) Reading Room. In 1913, the Yuè founded Píngmín (Ping Ming) Reading Room; the Fúzhóu founded Àiqún (Ai Chun) Reading Room; and the Hainanese founded Tòngwén (Tung Wen) Reading Room. Other reading rooms were also founded but their histories were obscure.[126]

Tax money was spent on Raffles Library. But the public library served few Chinese (or Malays, or Indians).

The Chinese started fifty reading rooms. The number included the United Chinese Library. These public clubs provided newspapers and other reading materials, and they provided educational opportunities for the poor. The desire to be able to read and write was strong among the illiterate and impoverished coolies, and these rooms attracted many.

Incidentally, the reading clubs served as liaison points for an anti-Manchu movement. Founded by Sun Yat-sen, the Tongmenghui infiltrated the Xīngzhóu Reading Room, and its leaders were the benefactors of the other reading clubs. The revolutionary group later formed the nucleus of the Guomindang.[127]

In response, the British authorities suppressed the reading clubs, which seemed perfectly reasonable. Except that they offered nothing in place of those reading rooms.

By the end of the First World War in 1918, thirty-nine modern Chinese schools were operating in Singapore. The number included girls' schools and night schools.[128]

The colonists had given education little consideration. The sudden change in political and social situation caused the government to stumble on the truth – that they were unable to control the education of most schoolchildren.

Up until the start of the 1919 Paris Peace Conference, European boys in Singapore were sent to schools in England, which aimed to foster administrators for the Colonial Service, while fee-paying Eurasians and Asians (children of Malay chiefs and wealthy Chinese merchants) were taught at local English schools, which aimed to produce junior civil servants.

Since education in English was the avenue to "sweatless livelihood"[129], it had to be limited for economic and political reasons[130]. And because children were expected to take up jobs where their parents worked, the school system mirrored colonial society in Singapore.

To make the remaining Malays better peasants and fishermen, they were instructed without charge at rural schools. The Tamils were taught at the plantations, and the Chinese were left to their own devices. Because the Chinese community ran their own schools, the government was unable to define educational content in these schools.

Nevertheless, even if there were simmering resentments, the sun had yet to set on the British Empire. And since opium revenue was shrinking, and since there were neither income taxes[131] nor capital-gain taxes to fund social services, and since it was not customary for colonizers to satisfy the colonized, the government picked themselves up off the hard truth and went on exploiting natural – as well as human – resources, as if nothing had happened.

Activism in Chinese Schools

As long as public peace was undisturbed, British authorities were indifferent to the changes at Chinese schools. After all, they regarded these schools as alien institutions.

The Peace Preservation Act (1867) already empowered the government to detain and deport seditious teachers. As a precaution, they took a further measure, enacting the Passenger Restriction Ordinance in April 1919. This would stop criminals and other undesirables from boarding ships at British treaty ports. Potential subversives, such as dissidents who were cracked down by the Beiyang government, would therefore be prevented from reaching the shores of Malaya, where they could find work as Chinese-school teachers. But the aftermath of the First World War provoked the Chinese living inside the borders of Malaya.

After the end of the First World War, the Allied victors held the Paris Peace Conference, which led to the Treaty of Versailles. The treaty did not return German concessions in Shandong to China, but transferred them to Japan. Failing to follow through the ideals of self-determination, the conference seemingly betrayed its own principles, and that led to student demonstrations in Beijing known as the May Fourth Movement.

The Movement influenced many Chinese in Malaya. Enraged by the situation, they were filled with resentment against the Japanese. Groups of workers and students went around town searching for Japanese goods to destroy. They forced Chinese households and shopkeepers to discard all Japanese goods.[132]

(Nevertheless, the boycott was not entirely based on Chinese nationalism. The Yuè and Kèjiā shops were importers and sellers of Japanese-made piece-goods; the Straits Chinese, British-produced piece-goods. And the China-born Mǐnnán were either importing from China or manufacturing piece-goods themselves in Singapore. At any rate, since Indian and Arab merchants continued to import and sell Japanese goods throughout the boycott, its success was uncertain.)[133]

The colonial government imposed a curfew and martial law, but the disturbances continued. Clashes erupted. Deaths resulted. After a while, open violence subsided, but the boycott continued. Threats ensured Japanese goods were not bought, sold, or handled by the Chinese. Anonymous letters of intimidation were sent. A Chinese shop selling Japanese goods was bombed. To meet the daily needs of the community, some schools encouraged the Chinese to make commonly used items themselves. The night session of Yangzheng School produced tooth-powder, ink, and shoe-polish.[134]

The British authorities arrested Chinese-school teachers, including the principal and a teacher from Ai Tong School. Also taken into custody were employees of Guómínbào (Kok Min Pao), a newspaper founded by the Guomindang five years earlier. The government found literary works with pro-China sympathies in Chinese schools, and they repatriated teachers with significant quantities of such possession.[135]

Chinese communities all over British Malaya found the banishments unwarranted, and they organized rousing sent-offs for the deportees. In Perak, hundreds of well-wishers, including students dressed in white as a sign of mourning, gathered to bid a teacher farewell. And in Singapore, the local Chinese community presented many gifts to the principal of Yangzheng School, while he was awaiting repatriation.[136]

Although these deportations restored order, tension between the government and the Chinese community heightened. First, Chinese schools were drawing students away from English schools. Next, the boycott and riots not only breached the peace but were also disruptive for business, and that undermined the economy and British interests.[137]

The final straw was the refusal to celebrate Allied victory in the First World War. The colonial government wanted crowds to gather in celebration at Raffles Reclamation Ground, and the schools to take part in the festivity. All went well until news of the Shandong problem reached the Chinese community. Its schools and the poor avoided the celebrations, showing resentment toward the colonists.[138] The British authorities became infuriated, and they quashed the growing nationalist sentiments in Chinese schools, the way imperial governments do.

In 1920, the Registration of School Ordinance was enacted to restrict the activities of Chinese schools. All schools were registered and subject to inspection. Chinese schools were classified as either "Modern", where the medium of instruction was in Mandarin, or "Old Style", where the mediums of instruction were in the regional dialects.[139]

In 1923, two new positions were created to tighten inspection and control: an Assistant Director of Education for Chinese Schools and an Inspector of Chinese Schools. Attempting to make these appointments palatable, the education department introduced a system of grants-in-aid for Chinese schools. But to qualify for the grants, the schools had to, first, accept regular inspections; second, include English education in their curriculum; and third, revert to teaching in non-Mandarin Sinitic languages. In 1932, although many schools were in need of monetary assistance, only 10 of the 215 registered Chinese schools applied for and got financial aid.[140]

In 1925, all teachers and school administrators were registered, and those found unregistered were punished. Schools were closed if its teachers and students were identified as Guomindang activists. Several were Hainanese schools.[141] The Guomindang was ordered to be closed. The organization dismantled itself, but kept its organizational networks and operated illegally.

In 1926, more schools were closed. Laws were also enacted to grant the government power to refuse registration for any – school, teacher, or school administrator – that was judged to be undesirable.[142]

In 1927, after the Guomindang successfully established the Nationalist government in China, the ban on its branches and activities in Singapore was lifted. In 1930, the ban was imposed again.

In 1933, the Aliens Ordinance was enacted. Since the Passenger Restriction Ordinance did not allow for migrants inside Malaya to be controlled, it was replaced by the new law, requiring alien residents, including teachers from China, to register themselves. Chinese-school teachers could then be tracked. And if found to be subversive, they were banished. New grant-in-aid to Chinese schools was also halted that year after a change in policy – funds were diverted to give free primary education in Malay.[143]

(The new policy triggered heated debates in the Legislative Council. In 1934, the governor rejected calls to give free primary education in English because of economic and political reasons.)

In 1935, teachers and textbooks from China were prohibited. Only teachers born in British Malaya were allowed to teach, and schools were permitted to use only locally published educational materials. But both policies were unrealized, since the education department could neither train teachers nor publish books for Chinese schools. Textbooks deemed detrimental to colonial interests were banned, and then replacement textbooks were allowed to be imported from China. Activities in Chinese schools were closely scrutinized.[144]

In 1936, grants-in-aid to Chinese schools was resumed, but the schools were required to show that they were teaching in the circumscribed syllabus. And at least six 40-minute periods of English-language lessons per week had to be given by a teacher with at least "Junior Cambridge" qualifications.[145]

In 1937, the Second Sino-Japanese War broke out. In 1938, Hitler seized Austria. In 1939, Britain entered the Second World War. In 1940, Japan formally joined the Axis Powers, automatically putting China on the side of the Allies. In 1941, the onset of the Pacific War forced the British to abandon their political controls. They recognized and accepted all political parties, including Guomindang and the Malayan Communist Party, and recruited the Chinese into Dalforce, a guerrilla unit commanded by a Special Branch officer, John Daley. The

Chinese themselves, however, called it the Singapore Overseas Chinese Anti-Japanese Volunteer Army.

British authorities tried achieving political ends in the face of deteriorating public sentiment. They were intolerant and discriminated against Chinese education. And that fomented skepticism among the Chinese, who developed an excessive distrust for successive governments after the Second World War.

To compound the problem, the pre-war colonial authorities placed a small English-speaking group, who monopolized the professions and government appointments, on the upthrow side of the Nanyang-Bukit Timah fault line, where Raffles College was located. Two earthshaking events, the Second World War and the Cold War, would later pile the Bukit Timah crustal plate on top of the Nanyang tectonic plate, where Nanyang University was going to be founded. This is known as orogeny in geology, and it is known to cause seismic upheaval in politics.

And another thing, in the forty years between 1873 and 1913, Singapore enjoyed unprecedented prosperity, expanding its trade eightfold, attracting immigrants from areas around the region, and inspiring the British authorities to become Lincolnesque. They abolished indentured immigration in 1914, but that decreased opium revenue and caused demographic changes in Singapore.

Demographic changes

Demographic changes in Singapore[147]			
Natural increase (decrease) of Chinese population		Net increase in Chinese immigration	
1881-91	(30,932)†	1881-91	74,798†
1891-01	(42,542)†	1891-01	88,522†
1901-11	(53,300)	1901-11	108,800
1911-21	(36,600)	1911-21	132,200
1921-31	9,600	1921-31	93,900
1931-47	176,500	1931-47	134,300
1947-57	395,600†	1947-57	112,200†‡

† figures include non-Chinese ethnic groups: Malays, Indians and others.
‡ migration gain was 141,400 from Peninsular Malaysia, but 29,200 left Singapore for countries other than Peninsular Malaysia.

The period between 1981 and 1921

Singapore was built on policies of free trade, open immigration, and zero insurance coverage. Coolies arrived. They carved notches on the wall, marking the days to the end of their indentured term, and dreamed of returning to their families and their lives in China. Some saved enough money and went home richer. Others changed their minds and settled down. A whole slew perished before fulfilling their contracts, from famine, from sickness, from opium overdose, or from occupational hazards, which may have included combat duties during clan wars. Nevertheless, some deceased got a funeral from their clan associations[146], and all would have found a deep burial in the hearts of their family, to whom their earnings were remitted. Many more Chinese died on the island than were born. (see above table)

The period between 1921 and 1931

Opposition to the practice of footbinding began around the late eighteen-nineties. At Guangdong Province, the Qing reformer Kang established the Canton [sic Yuè] Foot Emancipation Society. He asked his two daughters to unbind their feet, setting them as examples to influence its members. The members pledged to, first, leave their daughters' feet unbound; and second, disallow their sons to marry a girl with bound feet.

After a generation of anti-footbinding activism, leaders of the New Culture Movement promoted feminism. At around the time of the First World War, some Yuè women abandoned traditional values, leaving home to work in the sericulture industry. The feminist movement also led to more female emigration. An increasing number started going abroad to British Malaya, where they took up a variety of household jobs with the Europeans and wealthy Chinese families.

As more and more single maidservants found their right coolies, Chinese babies poured into Singapore (see above table) and Peninsular Malaysia (see below table).

Natural increase (decrease) of Chinese population in Peninsular Malaysia[148]	
1911-21	(1,014,208)
1921-31	(589,537)
1931-47	490,758
1947-57	366,885

The period between 1931 and 1947

To limit the immigration rate, the British authorities permitted only a fixed number of coolies to enter Malaya. They imposed the Immigration Restriction Ordinance from 1930, but applied it selectively to laborers from China.

But the government was eager to stabilize the violent Chinese community, and they did not count women and children towards the quota each month. They believed female and child immigration would transform the transient Chinese sojourner into a settled family man.

Most married coolies had endured long-distance conjugal relationships, and illiteracy made these sufferings worse. At both ends of their romantic correspondence, the man and his wife each paid a letter writer to compose and read out mail. Such days were over. With indentured labor contracts abolished and living together with their wives in British Malaya, indigent Chinese laborers sired even more babies. Lots and lots of them.

(When the Pacific War broke out in 1941, the colonial government suspended the Immigration Restriction Ordinance because they were mobilizing the Chinese for the defense of Malaya.)

In Singapore, as many as 176,500 more Chinese were born than died. The number who passed away included some 75,000[149] young men massacred during the Sook Ching. This was a Japanese military measure to exterminate what they considered to be hostile elements, through ethnic cleansing and decimating the Chinese community.

In Peninsular Malaysia, the natural increase of Chinese population also escalated in the same period of time. That was despite the number succumbing to disease and starvation, brutality and massacre in the hands of the Japanese.

The period between 1947 and 1957

Comprising 110,100 from Peninsular Malaysia and 29,200 from Singapore, as many as 139,300 more migrants left British Malaya than entered it.[150] Included among their number were those who journeyed back to the fatherland after the People's Republic of China was established. Instead of slaving away at the base of Malaya's economic pyramid, some chose to return to the promised land of reforms and redistribution.

Others had no choice but to remain in China. After visiting the communist country, they were refused re-entry by British authorities, who were worried about Maoist influence. Outcasts who were unable to return to their homes in the colony included students who were studying in China, as well as the founder of Chinese High School[151].

Despite a number leaving by their own volition, and despite disallowing British subjects who visited China from returning, and despite denying entrance to new migrants from the communist country, the Chinese population in Singapore kept growing. This increase was due to higher birthrates in Singapore, as well as inflows from Peninsular Malaysia, where the offspring of mining coolies and plantation workers reached adulthood.

As many as 366,885 more Chinese were born in Peninsular Malaysia than died. These children were born even under wartime conditions. Because they wanted to keep their insurance policies valid, the British termed the guerrilla war as the *Malayan Emergency*.[152] And because they wanted to justify their cause, the Malayan National Liberation Army (MNLA) called it the *Anti-British National Liberation War*.

The natural increase of 366,885 in Peninsular Malaysia would also have been greater if not for emigration. Some 251,500 more migrants left than entered the peninsula. The number comprised 110,100 departing for countries other than Singapore; and 141,400 for Singapore.[153]

Migration between the two territories under British rule was completely free. Hence, many, who were mostly in their teens and twenties, rejected the secret societies of their ancestors, leaving their homes in the tin mines and plantations, advancing their way down the peninsula, crossing the causeway for higher wages on the island, taking their obedient places in society, and aimed to become successful cogs in the labor movement.

Other offspring stayed back in Peninsular Malaysia. Some of them joined the Malayan Communist Party, a political machine with gears that meshed with the cogwheel of the trade unions.

Governmental inertia in meeting the increased needs of a growing population would force the mass into motion, activating the machinery of subversion by friction and tension – between the poor and the rich, between the colonized and the colonizers, and between the seekers of social justice and the stakeholders in the Rule of Law.

Notes:

The Straits Settlements, the Federated Malay States, and the Unfederated Malay States were three British possessions. Together, they are loosely termed as "British Malaya."

In 1946, the British brought the separate governments, excluding Singapore, together and placed them under a single authority. The merged entity was known as the Malayan Union, and it was later renamed the Federation of Malaya. The federation

---

and the Colony of Singapore were still British territories and remained as "British Malaya."

In 1957, "British Malaya" ceased to exist after the Federation of Malaya gained independence. Only the Colony of Singapore remained a British territory.

In 1963, the British gave up all their Southeast Asian possessions. Malaysia came into existence only after they added Singapore, Sabah (North Borneo), and Sarawak to the federation.

But out of convenience, I had used the term "Peninsular Malaysia" in the earlier passage to refer to a geographical territory, that of British Malaya excluding Singapore.

Chapter 4

● ● ● ● ● ● ● ● ●

JAPANESE OCCUPATION
Another Imperial curriculum

After Lt. Gen. Arthur Percival surrendered Singapore to Lt. Gen. Tomoyuki Yamashita at the Old Ford Motor Factory, the new government merged the four language streams into one – Japanese stream. The Japanese occupiers set up schools to teach various subjects, especially vocational courses that could help the armed forces in the repair of vehicles and equipment.

But with some schools destroyed and others closed and still others commandeered by the army, children thronged the streets, stealing and making trouble and adding to the disorder of the day. To get them off the streets and under control, these children were sent back to the schools they were attending before the war. The occupying power restored the racial and linguistic segregation set up by the British.[154] (Just like that.)

The US submarine campaign against Japanese shipping caused a lack of suitable textbooks. That, and a shortage of teachers who could speak Japanese, led many schools to resume teaching in the four languages. Chinese schools taught mostly Chinese and some Japanese; Malay schools, mostly Malay and some Japanese; Tamil schools, mostly Tamil and some Japanese, and government English schools, mostly English and some Japanese.[155]

Private English schools, the exception, were forced to stay closed.[156] No religious instruction could be given, lest the pupils forget how blessed were those who inhabited the dominions of the Rising Sun, for the emperor was the Son of Heaven.

With hunger and terror a constant threat, an untold number of disbelieving parents refused to send their children to school.

Chapter 5

• • • • • • • • •

POSTWAR TRANSITION
A new deal

Demographics were already changing in Malaya when the rampage began. In the state of anomie between the surrender of the Japanese and the arrival of the British, the Chinese pillaged and slaughtered the Malays in revenge[157]. The Malays rallied to defend themselves.

Before the Second World War, both the Malays and the Chinese had coexisted peaceably because the British treated both with equal condescension. The Japanese, however, created a new social order during their occupation. They governed the country with British-trained Malays, cultivating fanatical Malay nationalists and filling the constabulary with Malay volunteers. At the same time, they brutalized the Chinese. The Kempeitai, or mil-

itary police, used Malay constabulary to carry out puni-
tive measures on their behalf. These pro-Malay policies
filled the Chinese with animosity.[158]

After the Japanese surrendered the war, the British
took back their former territories in Asia. In Malaya and
British Borneo, members of the armed forces filled the
ranks of the interim administration. Without resolving
the underlying causes, these troops under the British
Military Administration (BMA) tried to stamp out racial
violence. They were determined to do whatever it took to
bring their territories back under British control and get
the situation back to normal, as before the war.

They fought a guerrilla war against the Malayan Communist Party. As part of the counter-insurgency effort,
British authorities corralled the rural Chinese population
into guarded camps, euphemistically termed "new villages."

The largest number of resettled Chinese was at Kinta,
a district of Perak some thirty miles away from historical
Larut. Kinta is also once famous for its tin. Why was
there such a large number of rural Chinese squatters in
Kinta? According to the popular opinion at that time,
many urban Chinese had migrated into rural areas to
avoid the Kempeitai during the Japanese occupation.
But some criticized this view because illegal Chinese settlements were already a problem before the war. In 1947,
the Perak Advisor on Chinese affairs attributed the
squatter situation to the immigration policy, which was
hastily contrived to deal with problems caused by the
economic slump in the nineteen thirties.[159]

Meanwhile, in an urban jungle three hundred miles away from Perak, unintended consequences from the Aliens Ordinance and the quota to restrict Chinese men also upset population patterns. "Chicks" of coolies in Singapore were similarly home to roost as if they were infestations of Xenomorph hatchlings. The below age-pyramid diagrams[160] illustrate the problem.

Age pyramids in Singapore

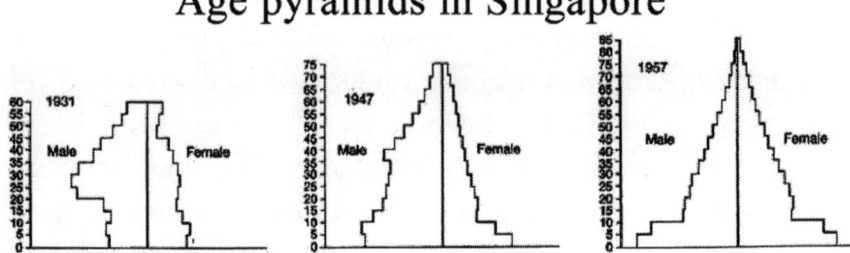

Total population: 0.56 million in 1931, 0.94 million in 1947, and 1.45 million in 1957.[161]

Even after passing the 1933 ordinance to register and control them, alien residents were regularly relocating themselves to improve their economic situation, since internal migration within British Malaya was completely free.

So, with the chop-chop haste of a post-production studio adaptation, the colonial government passed three immigration legislations[162] in the two years between 1952 and 1953, dismantling and reworking the Aliens Ordinance, and restricting British subjects from migrating into the peninsula[163]. In the context of the situation, the words "British subjects" can be interpreted to mean "Chinese who were born in the Straits Settlement."

This increase in population caused overcrowding. The number of people in Singapore escalated from 500-plus thousand (1931) to 900-plus thousand (1947) and kept on growing. Most people lived in the inner city, and many households were squeezed into one room or cubicle. Shop assistants slept on the floor after shops closed. In Chinatown, some shelves were hired out to day laborers at night and to night-shift workers during the day.[164]

The stress from living under such conditions pushed concerns of social injustice into the forefront of public debate. Although the problem had always existed, alien coolies attempting to achieve justice through violence were deported to China. But after the war, many victims of exploitation protesting the unfairness were born in Singapore, which is too small to set up a gulag camp.

Between the end of the Second World War and the end of the Korean War, continual inflation benefited those counting on their assets to increase in price. But it caused a fall in living standards among those using their muscles to make a living. Low wages, high unemployment, and population growth prodded the working class to get their union cards. Although it caused major disruptions to the economy, strikes were the usual way to improve their situation.

Set against this backdrop of social discontent and anti-British sentiment, the colonial authorities tried to overhaul Singapore's education system.

The Ten-year Plan

After the war, the colonial government finally accepted the principle of "education for all", introducing the Ten-year Plan in 1947. It promised six years of free primary school education for children from six to twelve years of age. Since there was no unemployment among those leaving the English secondary schools, a clamor for English education arose.[165]

The majority in Singapore could neither read nor write at that time. These illiterates made up sixty-three percent[166] of the population, and they envisioned their children to first pass from primary school through secondary school, then graduate with a coveted school certificate, and finally get a clerical job with the government or a sales job with a British company – even before their children were conceived. But when a great number of children were forced to leave school at the end of grade six, disappointment arose for them.

Since not enough school facilities were available to meet the expected demand, ten schools were scheduled to be built each year for ten years.[167]

As a stopgap measure until the new schools were built, the government retained the four-language system for uninterrupted enrollment.[168]

Before the war, meritorious students in Malay schools could transfer to English primary schools, and they were given intensive special training after the third grade to help them transition. Such transfers and special classes were to be extended to all vernacular schools.[169]

Parents were also given a choice of continuing their children's education in vernacular languages, if they wanted it.[170]

The education department planned to set up post-primary schools. These schools would charge fees and admit students who achieved a certain standard. Post-primary education in English would lead either to an Academic or a Technical course, and post-primary schools in the vernacular languages would teach vocational skills, preparing students for careers open to vernacular students. But there was no mention of what careers, other than teaching, were open to graduates of vernacular post-primary schools in Singapore.[171]

Teacher education

To meet the surging demand for teachers, the education department started the Teachers' Training College, and it acquired a building for that purpose. In the first year, the college trained 150 teachers for English schools and 40 more teachers for Chinese schools. But until it graduated its first cohort of students in 1950, teachers for secondary schools continued to be recruited from Raffles College.[172]

The management committees of the Chinese schools opposed the proposal, since they felt that local teachers trained at the college were unqualified.[173]

However, the communists took over China in 1949, and the colonial government disallowed any travel to China. To enter the Unified Education Service, teachers had to be trained full-time at the Teachers' Training College. That was the only acceptable qualification.[174]

The Supplementary Five-year Plan

Singapore's education department was providing free education for only 6,463 students at Malay schools in 1947, and they estimated that 100,000 pupils would eventually become eligible for free primary education. But later, the census found the population at around 941,000 in 1947. Residents under ten years of age made up over a third (33.3%) of the people in Singapore, and those under twenty made up more than half (50%).[175]

The British authorities took the new requirements into consideration when they introduced the supplementary five-year plan in 1949. The plan proposed to build eighteen more new primary schools each year for five years. Although they were to be simply and cost-effectively built, these schools would be serviceable, with just classrooms, administrative sections, and latrine blocks. As English schools were most in demand, only these were to be built under the supplementary plan.[176]

The progress update

The progress by the end of 1950. Eighteen schools under the five-year plan were completed. But only four schools under the ten-year plan started construction. After that, expansion slowed because inflation was so severe that it caused land prices, and building material costs, to soar.[177]

The progress by the end of 1952. Under the ten-year plan, only six schools out of the scheduled fifty were completed. Two more were still under construction. And under the supplementary plan, only thirty-two schools out of the scheduled fifty-four were completed. Net public expenditure on education was 13.2% of total government expenditure that year. It was only 5.5% when the ten-year plan was introduced in 1947.[178]

The decision in 1953. Constrained by the lack of money and overwhelmed by the sheer numbers of pupils, the deputy financial secretary announced that both plans would be discontinued.[179] When the Ten-year Plan and the Supplementary Five-year Plan ended, many were disheartened because they had counted on a free English education to get out of manual labor into a cushy nine-to-five clerical job.

Furthermore, problems with the primary schools had taken so much attention that the education department neglected building secondary schools. "Half-baked" students left primary school, without knowing enough to be employable, yet having learned enough to desist from a life of labor. Many became juvenile delinquents or targets of subversive propaganda.[180]

Perhaps the British authorities did things in the wrong order. In comparison, Stalin's five-year and Hua Guofeng's ten-year plans made more sense.

When the Chinese Communist Party came into power in 1949, its leaders aimed to transform China into a modern and powerful socialist nation. In economic terms, they mobilized all surpluses for industrialization.

By 1958, its farms and factories flooded the market. Foodstuffs and manufactured goods were extraordinarily cheap in Singapore. An attractively designed Chinese-made alarm clock costs only $2.50 (6s), and a five-valve hi-fi radio with three amplifier costs only $135 (£15 15s).[181]

China, which had bought rubber from Singapore, bartered rice for it in Indonesia. The Soviet Union also gave military aid to the anti-imperialist, pro-communist Sukarno government, in return for rubber and other agricultural produce.[182] The entrepôt was cut out of its intermediary role because the Cold War divided Asia and Europe into two geopolitical blocs – the "First" and "Second" Worlds.

To make the situation worse, the First World bought less tin and rubber from the British colony during the Eisenhower Recession. The bad timing of the sharp downturn hit Singapore hard because its economy lacked manufacturing industries to reduce unemployment.

The long-term forecast was also dismal because the birth rate was high.[183] With one baby born every eight minutes, the population grew to one-and-a-half million that year. In addition, more than one-third of those living in Singapore were still under the age of ten years, and more than half were under twenty.

Perhaps because the health minister was a Catholic, and because the populace was largely Chinese, the government was unable to square the pyramidal population structure.[184] The Labor Front administration found implementing birth-control policies painful.

And school leavers from the Federation of Malaya were looking for work at mills in the colony, piling up the grist higher and higher.

The chief minister said some commercial firms received more than a hundred applications for junior clerical jobs.[185] Only opium smokers might have dreamed of finding white-collar work.

"We are turning out more people every year with school certificates than needed," said the education minister. "There are no jobs for them. The school certificates may soon become as worthless as a scrap of paper."[186]

The Chinese-medium schools

While certificates from the English schools were destined to be worth nothing, credentials from the Chinese schools and some loose change couldn't get you a bus ride into town. It was then standard practice to buy tickets on busses with the Fúlǎo dialect, not with the language taught in Chinese schools. A poll[187], taken as late as 1979, found almost all Chinese passengers spoke the dialect with bus conductors, even if they were Malay or Indian; five percent of Malay and Indian passengers used it with Chinese bus conductors; and surprisingly, one-and-a-half percent of Malay passengers spoke Fúlǎo to Indian bus conductors.

Fúlǎo was also the language of commerce among the Chinese. It was spoken in the big-time boardrooms of the largest public companies and on the sidewalks, where salted-egg congee was sold from two suspended baskets balanced at the ends of a long bamboo pole across the shoulder of a small-time hawker.

Meanwhile, the Yuèhǎi language, not Mandarin, was spoken by the Chinese at government offices. Since the days of running the Chinese Protectorate, colonial authorities filled many low-skilled jobs, such as janitors and junior clerks, in their offices with Yuè people. That was probably because British officials who were posted from Hong Kong were more likely to speak Yuèhǎi than Fúlǎo or Mandarin, or probably because the "chief clerks" squeezed his relations and friends into such jobs, or a combination of both reasons. The time-honored tradition of family-based favoritism continued after the war.

Middle-ranking executive posts in the Straits civil, legal, and medical services were open to British subjects of all races from the nineteen-thirties, but few were admitted.[188] That's because very few qualified.

Some were those who had won the Queen's Scholarships to study in England. Launched in 1886, only one or two scholarships were given out each year to students from all British Malaya. These awards were discontinued in 1911 but restored in 1924, with only two granted each year. Between 1931 and 1934, three were awarded annually.[189] Scholarships were mostly bestowed on British residents and Eurasians at first. Nevertheless, the number of Malay and Straits Chinese recipients gradually increased. After a slow start, the Indians caught up before the scholarships were abolished, winning the last two in 1957. The non-Fúlǎo Chinese were under-represented every year.

Others were those whose parents had the means to send them abroad for further education, Among the Chinese, they were mostly children of wealthy Fúlǎo merchants.

The color bar reserved senior appointments for the colorless.

And so, in a typical government department, a creolized Yuèhǎi language was spoken among the janitorial and clerical class. Fúlǎo chitchats were found among the junior officers. Dialects, ranging from Scottish-English to Anglo-Cornish, were used to brighten the colorless language of the tuans besar, who allegedly faked an Etonian accent when British royalty visited Singapore.

Mandarin had no place in Singapore, nor the Straits Settlement, nor anywhere else in Southeast Asia for that matter, except perhaps in the jungles of Malaya.

Tertiary Education in Malaya

Three years after Prussia set up Tongji University in Shanghai, the British established theirs at Hong Kong in 1911. And eight years after the University of Hong Kong was founded, the Methodist Mission proposed to set up Anglo-Chinese College in Singapore. But the scheme was shelved after the colonial government opposed it.

After nine more years of waiting for a tertiary institution, Raffles College was finally founded. It opened its doors to forty-three students in 1928.

Sadly, the college was ran as an institution for training teachers[190], awarding only Diplomas of Arts or Science after three years of study. The value and recognition of its diplomas were a matter of contention.[191]

The McLean Commission investigated the state of higher education in 1938, concluding that the time was not ripe for Malaya to have a university. Three more commissions were appointed to make their studies in 1939, 1946, and 1947. The commission at each of those years found that it was still not the time for a university.

Still, the chairman of the last commission (Carr-Saunders) changed his mind the following year, and he supported the case to establish a university for Malayans.

In 1949, Raffles College was merged with King Edward VII College of Medicine to form the University of Malaya, finally clearing up any suspicion of foot-dragging.

Even more important, a university would also help placate the populace by conferring academic degrees. At once, the college was converted into a university, with no changes made to the faculty or student body. It was exactly the right time to form a university that year because the Malayan insurgency had started in 1948.

(The Teachers' Training College was founded in 1950 to replace Raffles College, the former academy for educating teachers.)

After the Second World War, the British attempted to meet the chronic demand for English-medium education, and tried to play down vernacular learning. Because public and aided schools were unable to meet the demand for education, private schools mushroomed. Many of these schools challenged the government.[192]

To control them, schools were registered, inspected, and given financial aid. Those not complying with regulation risked closure and withdrawal of subsidies. But the Education Department lacked inspectors to supervise Chinese schools. These schools were also unwilling to accept the conditions that were attached to the grants-in-aid.[193]

The government notified Chinese schools in 1951 that grants-in-aid would be reduced. As the ten-year plan and five-year supplementary plan progressed, subsidies would correspondingly be lessened. Once enough places were found for every student in English schools, financial aid would be completely withdrawn.[194]

But the public opposed vehemently, so the government shelved its plans to stop offering financial help for Chinese education. Under constant pressure, aid even increased the following year, in 1952. But by 1953, the British authorities were so overwhelmed by the demand for education that they made other plans to control vernacular educations. They increased the grants-in-aid still further, persuading the Chinese schools to follow regulations.[195]

Even though the government was unable to fund a universal English education, by 1954, the number of students at English schools exceeded those at Chinese schools. (see Fig 6)[196]

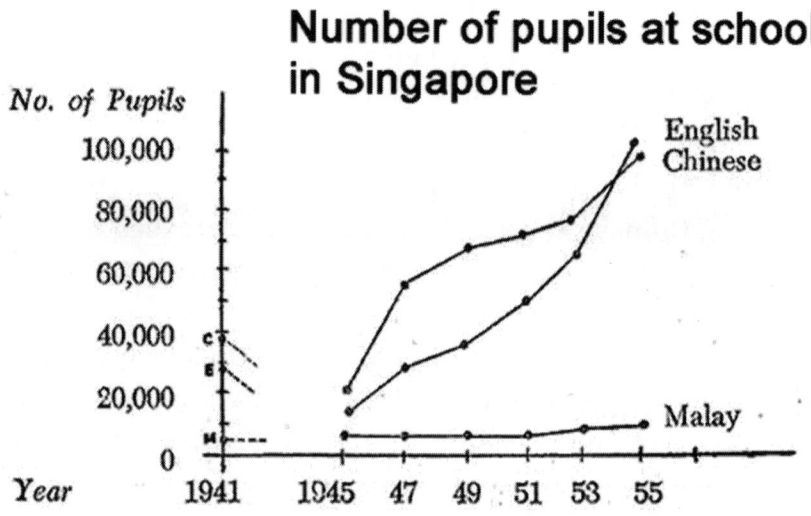

Number of pupils at school in Singapore

The colonial government tried to use education policies, the ten- and five-year plans, to draw pupils away from the Chinese schools, which they were unable to control, to the English schools, which they were able to control.[197] It was a fiendishly effective way to garner support from the poor, since indigent parents believed a free English education would get their children out of a life of labor. However, the ploy fell apart because British authorities failed to carry out their policy by want of money. All that effort ended in nothing, and worse.

For more than a hundred years, the colonial government empowered the Chinese-community leaders with the authority to oversee the Chinese population. Although the appointed representatives gained prestige, wealth, and stability, these policies fostered in them a conservative outlook. Young Chinese-educated intellectuals were paradoxically marginalized. When the government offered free English education, the leaders felt threatened.

Racial integration

Many local-born Chinese were clearly different from the traditional Straits Chinese. Although they were born and bred in Singapore, they spoke only Chinese and lacked ties with the rest of the inhabitants. The Chinese made up seventy-nine percent of the population, and the education of their children was going to decide the politics and culture of the future. Vernacular schools had perpetuated the barrier between the Chinese-speaking and the rest.[198] But it gave community leaders an intermediary role.

Since vernacular education produced socially disparate communities – each with its own language, interests, and cultural values – a common curriculum and a single language was needed to bridge them. The government attempted to instill the values of the English schools into the minds of vernacular-school students, helping them see the need for having shared values and a joint cultural heritage.[199]

This policy, however, frustrated both conservative leaders and marginalized intellectuals in the Chinese community.[200] They also feared cultural extinction, which was intensified by educational and political developments on both sides of the granite causeway.

Malaya's Barnes Report (1951)

A committee of Malays and Europeans put forward a proposal to develop a federal education system. It recommended using education to build up a common nationality, by providing six years of primary-school education in Malay and English. Members of the committee hoped Chinese and Tamil schools would wane and disappear over time.

The education director in Singapore, A. W. Frisby, said that that was exactly what they were trying to do in the colony.[201]

The Chinese community in Malaya opposed the recommendations. Although they agreed that Malay was the principal language, they felt that the British proposal should also have included Chinese and Tamil as part of the national identity.

Malaya's Fenn-Wu Report (1951)

The report noted that western culture was unsuitable for fusion, so forcing a merger would lead to further cleavage. Since the Chinese largely accepted the value of learning Malay and English, the committee recommended trilingualism for Chinese students and bilingualism for others. The Chinese affairs secretary in Singapore, Edward C. S. Adkins, was assigned to make these recommendations into a workable policy, which could be used in both the federation and Singapore.

Malaya's Education Ordinance (1952)

The Malays rejected the Fenn-Wu Report. So the colonial government implemented the Barnes Report's proposal for English-medium schools in the federation, over Chinese protests.

Singapore's All-Party Committee (1955)

Since the Colony of Singapore did not commission either the Barnes or the Fenn-Wu report, they made no formal decision to accept either reports. But strong reactions from the local press, from the Chambers of Commerce, and from the representatives in the legislature, forced them to review Chinese education. The Singapore government formed a committee.

The committee members were all elected assemblymen. They aligned themselves with the people and criticized the colonial government and their education policy. The program in the English schools revolved around Great Britain and its colonial possessions, which was a splendid red on the map. (see Fig 8.[202]) China was a disgusting snot-colored beige.

The all-party committee also objected to the curriculum at the Chinese schools. As shown on the map in Fig 7, Chinese schools were centering their education on civilization in the Middle Kingdom, whose borders were surrounded by barbarians. (The 1532 map[203] shown on Fig

7, is titled "World Diagram of China and the Barbarians.")

Their report, which was released in 1956, proposed that Chinese schools be transformed into local institutions and be treated the same way as the other schools. But Chinese schools had to discard many subjects about China and its culture. These institutions ought to have had a localized syllabus, one that first teach about Singapore and Malaya; next, their immediate neighbors; then, Asia; and finally, the rest of the world.[204] In other words, the world ought to have been viewed from the little red dot.

Torn between gratification and anxiety, the Chinese-educated community gave the committee report a mixed reception. They were sanguine over some suggestions, such as increasing subsidies and raising salaries for teachers at the Chinese schools, but were apprehensive about other recommendations, such as tightening control over management and improving the quality of English-language teaching.[205]

Malaya's Razak Report (1956)

The report was a compromise between the Barnes and Fenn-Wu reports, championing Malay as the main language of instruction. But it accepted the continued use of vernacular languages in education, including English.

Malaya's Education Ordinance (1957)

The Federation of Malaya gained independence in 1957. Alien residents who were born on the peninsula were given Malayan citizenship. The rest, including Singapore-born British subjects, were regarded as local residents.

And the newly independent country adopted the Razak Report for its educational framework.

The Eisenhower Recession (1958)

The recession in the United States had a disastrous effect on the economies of both Malaya and Singapore.

Malaya's Immigration Ordinance (1959)

Malaya passed a new immigration ordinance in May 1959 to safeguard the employment and livelihood of its residents.

As stated in the legislation, the wives (and children aged six and more) of local residents who had lived separately from their husbands (and fathers) for five continuous years after December 1954 were prohibited from entering Malaya. This would "bring about a more balanced and assimilated Malayan population [with] ties and loyalty to [...] a true Malayan nation."[206]

The 1959 law seems to be aimed at children of school-going age. Even though free education under the ten- and five-year plans was phased out in 1953, many parents from the peninsula continued to send their children to the remnant British colony perhaps because they were circumventing Malaya's 1952 and 1957 education ordinance, or perhaps because more jobs were open to school leavers in the city, or even perhaps because urban schools at the southern end of the causeway were seen to be better than rural ones.

Wives of non-citizens also appear to be targets of the ordinance. These women had lived for long periods away from Malaya. After taking their children across the causeway, they stayed to look after the minors, who were receiving an education on the patch of land off the tip of the peninsula.

Parachute kids and péidú māmā (study mothers) existed long before the words for them came into use. And I would also like to point out that astronaut families were being formed ahead of Yuri Gagarin's historic journey into outer space.

Singapore's Immigration Ordinance (1959)

The next month, the colony was granted full internal self-government, and from June that year, both its alien residents and its British subjects (citizens of the United Kingdom and Colonies) became British subjects (citizens of the State of Singapore).

Singapore's unemployment rate was 13.5% that year. So its new government couldn't wait to reciprocate the favor, passing their own immigration ordinance a short time later. The legislation was similarly an effort to safeguard the employment and livelihood of residents on the city island.

Malaya's Rahman Talib Report (1960)

The report recommended using Malay in all educational institutions, especially at tertiary level. That would quicken the process of national integration on the peninsula.

Malaya's Education Act (1961)

While Gagarin orbited Earth, the Rahman Talib Report was incorporated into the new law, stalling the space race by dampening enthusiasm for sending satellite children to schools on that (expletive deleted) island.

Formation of Malaysia (1963)

A hundred and forty-four years after Singapore was founded, its prime minister, Lee Kuan-yew, declared it an independent country, marking the end of British rule. And the new nation, together with Sabah and Sarawak, formed the Federation of Malaysia with its northern neighbor.

Don't be deceived by appearances though. Both governments – on the island and on the peninsula – tolerated migratory crossings over the top of the causeway, but swept their differences underneath.

Independence of Singapore (1965)

After joining the federation for less than twenty-three months, the State of Singapore was unexpectedly ousted from Malaysia.

Although education problems in both countries were connected to some extent, the newly independent republic took an approach that differed greatly from the federal system. On August 9, 1965, students at both ends of the causeway found their education path forked. For good.

Chapter 6

• • • • • • • • • •

PAP YEARS
On the trail of social democracy

A group of thirty-nine men and four women, in their party uniform of white-on-white, filed into City Hall on the afternoon of June 3, 1959, to witness their leader, Lee Kuan-yew, being sworn in as prime minister by the former governor and newly-appointed Yang di Pertuan Negara (Head of State), William Goode. The next day, they freed political detainees[207], and in another day, they trooped back into City Hall to witness the swearing-in of the remaining cabinet members.

They took their places at the Legislative Assembly, occupying forty-three seats out of fifty-one; and then the People's Action Party (PAP) focused on solving Singapore's economic and social problems, including education.

The government ratified the All-Party Committee Report, treating education in all languages – Malay, Chinese, Tamil, English – equally. They upgraded Chinese-medium school buildings and resources, sending their teachers for training at the Teachers' Training College. The labor ministry permitted Chinese-school teachers to organize unions, and the education ministry appointed supervisors who were acquainted with Chinese education.[208]

All pupils received free primary education. Malay was made the national language, since the newly elected government wanted Singapore to be part of Malaysia. But integration between the different races would be achieved with bilingual education. Or even trilingual education for some.[209]

From 1959 to the end of 1965, the government built 72 new schools, both primary and secondary. Education was free so that there was no discrimination between the rich and the poor.[210]

Parents were able to decide for themselves what language medium they wanted their children to study in[211], but this time there was no rush for English education.

To make the four-language education system consistent for all students, the four different streams had to teach a uniform set of values, and all schools had to prepare students for common national examinations. For the first time, the Primary School Leaving Examinations (PSLE) was extended to the vernacular languages in 1960.[212]

All six-graders sat for the PSLE in November that year, choosing to take the examination in any one of the four official languages. To make their mark on educational history, 32%[213] of students from the Chinese schools failed their examination. But it was the scholastic failures from the English schools who took center stage, since they made up an unbelievably defiant 66%[214] of those who sat for the English-medium PSLE. No wonder there was no clamor for English education.

With more students failing than passing their examinations, even at primary levels, English-medium education was not always preferred. For those who were going to drop out of school at an early age, it was more worthwhile to first give them a little Chinese education, and then send them for apprenticeship with a butcher, a baker, or maybe a secret-society troublemaker.

English-medium education, however, was favored by those with networking connections, or guānxi, to secure janitorial jobs with the government. So the Yuè Chinese, who called themselves Guǎngfǔ, were more keen to send their children to English-medium schools than the Fúlǎo. This comparatively greater enthusiasm continued well into the nineteen-seventies[215].

Perhaps, except those of Dabu and Meixian ancestry, the Kèjiā Chinese assimilated themselves into the Yuè and Fúlǎo community, some by marriage and others by associating their ancestry with Guangdong or Fujian provinces.

The Hainanese were shut out of guānxi networks. For this reason, they were more eager than the others to engage in communist activities.

When Singapore became completely self-governing in 1959, the unemployment rate was 13.5%. Its immigration law was amended to give only Singapore citizens the right to enter the country.

When Singapore merged with Malaysia in 1963, it doubled the size of the domestic market, and import-substituting industrialization created new jobs. However, the unemployment rate remained about 10%.[216]

After Singapore became independent in 1965, the government added an immigration checkpoint at Keppel Railway Station and another at its end of the causeway. That stopped unending lines of unlawful immigrants from streaming across the Strait of Johore, by trains and busses, on foot and bicycles. (Singapore had only air- and sea-based checkpoints in the past.)

Second, they re-registered citizens and residents, replacing their identity cards with newly designed ones to deter forgery and photo substitution.

Third, they implemented birth control policies.

But the quintessential factor that lowered the unemployment rate was export-led industrialization. By 1978, the unemployment rate was reduced to 3.6%. Companies that export were mostly financed with foreign capital and ran by foreign management, who rated academic qualifications and English-language competence more importantly than guānxi. So parents gradually stopped sending their children to vernacular schools.

In 1959, English schools enrolled only 47% of all children for primary one classes; Chinese schools, 46%; Malay and Tamil schools, the remaining 7%. Twenty years later in 1979, English schools enrolled 91% of all primary-one children, but Chinese schools enrolled only 9%. Malay- and Tamil-school enrollments were negligible.[217]

The Chinese Secondary Schools

Chinese middle schools were reorganized. The education program at the English-medium secondary schools was duplicated at the Chinese schools, including in 1961, instituting a national examination for tenth-graders at the end of secondary four. Only successful candidates could continue with two more years of study leading to a pre-university qualification.

Up until then, students at Chinese middle schools, after three years of study, were automatically promoted to high schools, where they would graduate after studying for three more years. Unhappy with the changes, they boycotted the Chinese School Certificate examinations, making a collective cry of defiance.

Warned that their children were going to waste one year of study, parents escorted their children through pickets into examination centers.

Integration of Schools

The government believed that uniting the different communities starts at the schools, where socially cohesive programs were implemented and equal opportunities given to all. But until then, only English-medium schools were ethnically diverse. Vernacular schools drew students from a single race.

To integrate students from different ethnic groups, the government placed two or three different streams into one school, which came under a single principal. These integrated schools taught English- and Chinese-stream classes, or English- and Chinese- and Malay-stream classes.

But the integration was unsuccessful because the only common language was English. Vernacular branches were perceived to be grafted into the English vine. Principals, teachers, and students from the English-stream, however, did not try to allay this ill-will, as they believed their social groups were superior, going back to the colonial days when the British were behind them.

The postwar Marxist class consciousness shifted into a division between the English- and Chinese-educated. The former was accused of elitism, their views carried more weight and their wisdom make them especially fit to govern, while the latter was accused of chauvinism, threatening racial harmony by pushing the values of Chinese culture.

Bilingualism

The monolingual education policy of the British led to political chaos after the Second World War. The turmoil continued through the merger years when Singapore was part of Malaysia. Everyone had the same opinion – rectify the colonial legacy with bilingualism.[218]

The government instituted an official policy of bilingualism, making second language compulsory for all primary schools in 1960, and extended the policy to secondary schools in 1966. Three years later in 1969, students sitting for the GCE O-level examination had to include the second-language subject. Four years later in 1973, they increased the weighting for the second-language at PSLE from 20% to 33.3%, and they reduced the first language weighting from 40% to 33.3%. The math and science weightings were each reduced from 20% to 16.7%.[219]

Families that spoke English or Mandarin or both at home possessed an advantage with bilingualism. Provided they desired it, some were better resourced to capitalize on their advantage. The prime minister sent his children to Chinese schools, but arranged for British voluntary service officers to read them English novels and poems weekly.[220] Of those sitting on the management committees of Chinese schools, a number of community leaders sent their scions and scionettes to English schools, but gave them Chinese lessons in the afternoon[221], since a towkay who neither read nor wrote Chinese is like the Tower of Pisa, with its foundation rooted in Latin and not in the people and culture of China.

Plebeians were exhorted to encourage their progeny to continue the tradition of Confucian scholarship. At first, hawkers, trishaw riders, washerwomen, and other commoners expected their offspring to leave school before reaching the last grade of primary education, and so were more likely to place them in the Chinese stream. But as their children started to get better grades, transitioning successfully from primary to secondary schools, the enrollment in Chinese schools declined. That was especially so because the economy was increasingly based on foreign investment. It conferred more opportunities for English-stream school leavers and changed the price of prejudice.

Perhaps this prejudice started in February 1930. The Straits Chinese were then proud of their elite status and responsibilities under British rule, but at the same time, they were also inspired by China's national awakening. Meanwhile, the authorities were suppressing the Guomindang in British Malaya. To warn their leaders to end "subversion", the governor summoned them to Government House. He upbraided a judicial officer, who simultaneously held his colonial appointment and involved himself in Guomindang activities, and insinuated that he was a double-headed snake serving two masters. He denounced the Straits-Chinese Guomindang leaders for wavering between England and China, pressuring them to make a choice.[222]

That choice was personified by the first two Queen's scholars of Asian descent in British Malaya.[223]

The *1887* recipient, Lim Boon-keng, was recognized with an OBE in 1918. He was the president of both the Guomindang (Singapore branch), from 1913 to 1914, and Xiamen (Amoy) University, from 1921 to 1937.

The *1888* recipient, Song Ong-siang, was recognized with a CBE in 1927. He stayed in the British camp and was knighted in 1936 – some six years after Cecil Clementi insinuated that Teo Eng-hock, the aggrieved judicial officer, was a "leung t'au sha."

At a top Chinese middle school, he used to teach the best class, where students were eager to learn and laughed at his puns and were responsive and positive. Over the years, smaller and smaller enrollments at primary one reduced the number of applicants to his middle school. The school had to increase its admission rate. Lately, students in the best class were merely above average.

Still worse, Lǎoshī (Teacher) was just transferred from the Chinese school to an integrated school, where he was asked to teach both first- and second-language classes. Like bricks, second-language students just sat at their chairs, staring blankly at him, and found everything above their heads.

Yet, he was more fortunate than colleagues who were posted to some mission schools for boys. Those brats pretended to pay attention in second-language classes, when in fact they were reading something else under their desk. Some allegedly fell asleep during lessons and left pools of drool on their desks. Heavens! That's enough to make an atheist turn to God. He reviled at the thought, and a wave of haughtiness swept over him. Who was the patron deity for teachers anyway? he sneered, as he ran his finger over the spines of well-thumbed books, books that were stacked on his bookshelf and were works of celebrated author Lu Xun and others from the League of Left-Wing Writers. They sparked an immediate surge of memory.

Fifteen years earlier in 1956, in strife to save Chinese education, he had taken part in a series of Chinese middle-school riots, suffering truncheon blows and jumping into Zhongzheng Lake to relieve himself from tear gas. Twice, he was locked up at police stations, his spirits defiant and undefeated by both arrests.

But now things were different. Tears welled as he sat down to fire yet another diatribe to the Chinese press, lambasting the government for abandoning a 2,500-year heritage – Confucius – and traditional Chinese culture.

In May 1971, four editors and journalists for the Nanyang Business Daily were arrested, under the Internal Security Act.

Chapter 7

• • • • • • • • • •

NANYANG UNIVERSITY
Rebels with a cause

Students from Nanyang University and the University of Malaya were as different as soldiers and pawns in xiàngqí and chess.

On a xiàngqí board is a grid of nine vertical and ten horizontal lines, and the lines that run across the board are known as ranks, numbering one (closest) through ten (farthest). The eight rows of squares on a chessboard are also called ranks.

Symbolic images for

**the 1949 student at
University of Malaya****the 1956 student at
Nanyang University**

A soldier (zú) moves one point along the line each time. It is "demoted" if it approaches the other end of the board. At the seventh and eighth rank, it is deemed a high soldier (gāo-zú) because it is more useful. But at the ninth and tenth rank, it is regarded as a low soldier (dī-zú). Since soldiers cannot retreat, they are set up early to trap and hinder opposing horses (bié-mǎ-tuǐ), and deployed later to obstruct hostile elephants (sài-xiàng-yǎn).

A chess pawn generally moves one square forward at a time, but it is promoted if it reaches the last rank of the chessboard. Chess games often end with a pawn race, where the goal is to get promoted first and win the game.

After the Second World War, the British returned as the lawful authority of Malaya. At the same time, the titular rulers (Malay Royalty) and the ruled (including the descendants of Malay fishermen, Chinese coolies, and Indian estate workers) were also asserting their rights in the land of their birth. Imposing British rule in the same manner as before the war was unacceptable, and the colonizer had to scramble for social, political, and economic advantages against the colonized. The race was on.

For the first time, in 1949, the colonial government held elections for the Municipal Commission, later renamed the City Council, giving some semblance of political freedom. In 1955, they formed the Legislative Assembly to grant more power to the local populace. The number of elected representatives was gradually increased from 1949, but it took six years for elected assemblymen to outnumber the nominated ones.

Also with enough haste to ward off outbreaks of seven-year itches, they localized the civil service by installing

Asians in the government. They had set up the University of Malaya to train locals for higher bureaucracy in 1949. And once they recognized that self-governance (and later independence) was unavoidable, they started another campus of the university at Kuala Lumpur so that more locals could be recruited into the administration. They readied the forthcoming government to take over Her Majesty's Government, which was going to leave Malaya.

But they expected the post-colonial government to support Britain, or at least expected it not to nationalize their commercial assets. They had outlawed, in 1948, those who were in the resistance movement against Japanese occupation. They drove their communist allies underground.

After years of fighting, they granted independence to the Federation of Malaya in 1957, depriving the insurrection of its justification as a war of colonial liberation. With no rationale for armed struggle, the communists retreated to the Malayan–Thai border.

When Indonesia challenged the creation of Malaysia in 1963, the *former colonizer* provided most of the defensive effort. In the three years of confrontation in Borneo, they covertly went on the offensive, inserting British infantry units and Commonwealth special forces into Kalimantan. That put their foes on the defensive and prevented the Indonesians from attacking when and where they chose. British casualties in Operation Claret were publicly reported as being incurred in Sabah or Sarawak, but no Malaysian soldier seems to be wounded or killed in action.

In 1968, they returned to take up arms against the Malayan Communist Party, who started a second insurgency after the Tet Offensive in Vietnam. They continued to fight the armed rebellion even after they closed their Singapore military bases. The Second Malayan Emergency lasted twenty-one years and ended in 1989, when the Maoists suspended hostilities, signed a peace agreement with the Malaysian government, and disbanded.

Nanyang University was the first Chinese university founded outside Greater China. Its Mandarin name, Nányáng Dàxué, is abbreviated to Nándà, or Nantah, based on the phonetic system used in Singapore during the nineteen-fifties.

The university was brought about by the charitable spirit of business owners, and its graduates were not expected to replace the towkay patriarchs when they leave this world. It also aroused opposition from both British officials, who were certain it hindered national integration, and Malay nationalists, who believed it obstructed efforts to create a Malay nation, Bangsa Melayu.

After the colonial government rejected the application for its registration, Nanyang "University" was incorporated in 1953 as Nanyang University Limited, a company under the Companies Ordinance. Its founders had no legal authorization to run an educational institution, and they would later be accused of chauvinism or abetting communism or both.[224]

Nantah started preparatory classes in 1955, the year Singapore was granted limited self-government but not independence. In the following year, it enrolled its first cohort of 584 students from that preparatory class into the Arts, Science, and Commerce faculties.

Two months later in May 1956, the education minister announced that the government was not going to recognize the university's degrees, as the institution had "no right to confer degrees."[225]

(Some churches in Singapore ran colleges, granting degrees that are also unacceptable by the civil service or commercial enterprises. But since these churches provided employment for their college graduates, they were permitted to set up their own seminaries, which are still running legally to this day.)

Nevertheless, Singapore's 1958 Constitution brought about events that helped change Nantah's destiny. The new constitution would come into force after the next general election, and it would make Singapore completely self-governing. The Legislative Assembly was going to be filled only with representatives who were elected at the general election of the following year.[226]

Desperate to win the election, Singapore's second chief minister, Lim Yew-hock, presented the Nanyang University Bill that year as he hoped for Chinese support at the ballot box. He offered accreditation if academic standards satisfy a committee of external assessors.

Mindful that the electorate at the next general election was going to be overwhelmingly Chinese, no political party dared to oppose the proposal. Every representative in the Legislative Assembly fervently declared their support.[227]

Like the others in the opposition benches, Lee Kuan-yew also supported the bill, but circumscribed himself by noting that sixty percent of Nantah's students were from the federation, whose government neither recognized the university nor subsidized these students. He also warned of vote-getting ploys and the need for assemblymen to consider future implications.[228]

When the assessors arrived in February 1959, the bill had already passed its second reading and the select committee. That pre-empted their work. The team submitted their findings on March 12, but the incumbent government did not make it public because the report was pessimistic.[229]

At the general election, the People's Action Party won the majority of the legislative seats and formed the next government. The new government released the Prescott Report to the public and appointed another committee for a second assessment.

But four hundred students was going to graduate in December, making history as the first Nantah graduates, and the newly elected prime minister, Lee Kuan-yew, could not afford to wait for the second opinion. He acted quickly.[230]

Four months after being sworn into office, the prime minister visited the Chinese university in October, giving a speech to one thousand students. He offered seventy government jobs to would-be graduates from the Class of 1960, which was more than the number taken from University of Malaya each year. Most of the seventy would enter the education service, and suitable graduates were also going to be given scholarships for postgraduate studies abroad, particularly in science and engineering.[231] The rest, three hundred and thirty graduates, personified an emerging social problem.

Previously, few students from Singapore studied at universities in China. When Xiamen University was founded in 1921, it was the only university that admitted students from outside China. Out of its first cohort of 120 students that year, less than half were from Southeast Asia. The second university admitting foreign students was Jinan National University, established in 1927. In 1929, the university had 775 foreign students[232], mostly from Indonesia, Malaya, and Thailand. But not all 775 were undergraduates. At that time, Jinan National University also operated a primary school, a middle school, and a high school within its campus.[233]

In those days, although students could continue their studies at a university in China, only those who were economically privileged were able to do so. Most high-school graduates in Singapore were "normal-trained" to become teachers. The upsurge in enrollment at Chinese schools, as well as the increase in the number of years that students spent in education, had kept demand for Chinese-school teachers high.

With the founding of Nanyang University, a great number of students were graduated. Even with accreditation, privately held European companies would hire only its bilingual graduates. Chinese businesses, mostly smaller enterprises with family and clan obligations, were unable to give enough opportunities for the rest.

The second committee to review Nantah finished its investigation in November, and they released their opinion when the legislative assembly was in session on February 6, 1960. The Gwee Ah-leng Report was also unfavorable.

Many disaffected graduates became left-wing radicals.

Nanyang University was founded during a time of social and political awakening in Malaya. The rise of anti-colonial sentiments forced the British authorities to give the people, first, municipal representation; next, legislative representation; then, limited self-governance; after that, complete self-governance; and finally, independence. They introduced a system of education that taught mainly in English for national integration, after having divided students by race for more than a hundred years.

Before the Second World War, the British had framed education policy to uphold colonial administration, which governed by dividing the population into communal groups and ruling through their leaders.

After Singapore merged with the federation, Malay nationalists also wanted a common language for integration and national identity, but based it on a universal education in the Malay language.

Both British officials and Malay leaders wanted to end Chinese education, and to have Chinese children assimilated into Malayan society. The Chinese community fought for the survival of Chinese schools in the education system, and Nantah, at the vanguard of these schools, became a symbol for that cultural and political struggle. Consequently, little importance was placed on academics or graduate placement.

Accomplished vice-chancellors, one after another, were appointed to office at the university, each with a specific plan and a distinct conviction, but the number achieving important and consequential change was exactly none. Those who tried to revamp academic programs, for the sake of preparing students for employment success, were berated for selling out to the other side. Those championing the grievances of the Chinese-educated community got popular ovations, but left themselves open to charges of chauvinism. Nanyang Avenue was littered with roadkills, caused by aggressive and agenda-driven criticism.

(The old Nanyang Avenue, a remote road leading to the front gates at the south end of the campus, was demolished. It was replaced by another road with the same name, and this leads to the current main entrance at the eastern side of Nanyang Technological University, an English-medium university inaugurated in 1991.)

During a series of riots in 1964, thirty-six people were killed and more than five hundred were injured in the State of Singapore, triggering a separation between the island and the peninsula the next year. In 1965, the government of the new Singaporean republic assured its people that, first, Malay remains the national language; second, schools would continue to teach in four official languages – English, Malay, Chinese, and Tamil – and students could choose to study in one of these languages; and third, ethnic integration was going to be realized through bilingualism, not assimilation.

To avert another race riot, any Chinese leader bringing culture to the fore as a political issue, or Malay leader pressing for increasing use of Malay, would be severely punished or criticized. Once racial and linguistic zealotry was restrained, the battle to save the university from decline advanced quickly. Few were as willing as the prime minister to pay the price for raising academic standards.

Money from the public purse was given to Nanyang University for academic reforms, including S$1 million to buy scientific equipment and another S$1 million to build a library. State funds paid for the construction and equipment of language laboratories. The government also paid for the running of English-language classes. Since 1964, bursaries worth half a million dollars were given to students each year.[234]

At the convocation ceremony in 1968, the education minister announced that he was satisfied with the restructuring, and that Singapore's government would, from that point on, recognize the degrees of Nanyang University. The entire graduating class of 1968 yelled in jubilation.[235]

The government, in their strife for academic excellence, constantly paid out of taxpayers' pockets, more bursaries and scholarships, facilities and staff salaries. By 1977, S$11.55 million was disbursed. The university consolidated its progress achieved hitherto and responded to changes in the labour market. In 1970, it started a graduate school, and in 1975, it introduced bi-lingual teaching[236], an effort about as effective as arming HMS Prince of Wales more heavily, for taking on an aerial assault.

No airlines fly directly from Singapore to Taiwan dur-ing the nineteen-fifties. The first Malayan Airways flight to a destination outside Southeast Asia was to Hong Kong in 1958, using a Douglas DC-4 leased from Qantas. To travel with multiple connections on propeller-driven airliners was slow, uncertain, and expensive. But jetting to Songshan Airport on a Boeing B747 during the nine-teen-seventies was fast, reliable, and affordable.

Second, the Guomindang, who established a refugee camp on the former Formosan Republic in 1949, trans-formed Taiwan into an industrial power. By the nineteen-seventies, the Republic of China had the second fastest-growing economy in Asia after Japan. Many of its foreign students graduated and found employment in the coun-try.

Third, because the republic was an ally of the United States during the Cold War, Washington supplemented ROC's education expenditure. By 1965, more than US$10 million, and another NT$735 million, was dis-bursed into various educational and cultural projects.[237] Based on the exchange rates of New Year's Day, 1965, the total for both amounted to about S$88 million. To encourage overseas Chinese enrollment, grants to Tai-wanese universities were allocated in proportion to the number of foreign students admitted. Foreign students without adequate Chinese language skills were given supplementary courses.[238] As Nantah was unable to match the competition by lowering tuition fees for foreign students, or improving faculty recruitment, it fought a losing battle against universities on the larger island.

After Indonesia and Malaysia gained independence and marginalized their Chinese-medium schools, wealthy Chinese from these countries continued to give their children a Chinese education. During the nineteen-fifties, they sent their offspring abroad to Chinese High School and Nanyang University. During the nineteen-seventies, they sent their children to schools and universities in Taiwan. After graduating from Taiwanese universities, many of these overseas-Chinese students pursued further studies in the United States. They chose American postgraduate institutions not only for their advanced degrees, but also for the opportunities to improve their English-language skills.

Even within Singapore, Chinese-stream students changed their preferences.

When the Straits and Federated Malay States Government Medical School was founded in 1905, Chinese-school students were denied places at the college. After the medical school was renamed King Edward VII College of Medicine, and after Raffles College was founded, they were still without exception rejected at both colleges. After both colleges were merged and upgraded into the University of Malaya in 1949, the discriminatory policy continued. No matter how deserving, Chinese-school students had to further their studies elsewhere.

From elsewhere to nowhere. After the communist took over China in 1949, Singapore's government changed its immigration laws, prohibiting students who were studying at the people's republic from returning to the colony.

(At that time, entry into and passage out of the people's republic was still permitted, so students from Indonesia and Thailand continued to study in China. The Chinese side of the Bamboo Curtain was locked down only during, and after, the Cultural Revolution.)

The need to offer higher education for Chinese-school students in Malaya led to demands for a Chinese university.

But the University of Malaya (Singapore division) started admitting Chinese-stream students from 1960. It started preparatory English courses for these students.

The government also gave top Chinese-stream students scholarships to study at overseas universities. By the nineteen-seventies, most students from Chinese schools preferred either to enroll at the English-medium university, then renamed University of Singapore, or to study abroad.

Consequently, Nanyang University was able to enroll only local students who were unable to qualify for the former or afford the latter.

The number of students studying at Chinese schools between 1945 and 1954, was more than the number at English schools. Nantah was therefore able to claim that admission to its 1955 preparatory class was more selective than the University of Malaya that year.

Because of the relentless fall in demand for Chinese-medium education, many primary and secondary schools were forced to change its language of instruction. Ninety percent of all children, who were registered in

1977 to start school at primary one, would enroll the following year into English-stream schools. That further exacerbated Nantah's woe.

Ngee Ann College was another attempt at establishing a Chinese-medium university. Located in the Teochew Building at Tank Road, it offered four-year degree courses.[239]

The college was founded in 1963. But the Cháoshàn foundation was less moneyed than the Fujian guild hall, which counted among its members many people of non-Fúlǎo ancestry.[240]

Three years after its founding, in 1966, they shambled to the government for grants, ceding control of the college to an independent council. Ngee Ann College introduced diploma courses for commerce and engineering that year. Its technological courses were most popular among students as Singapore was then industrializing rapidly, but that required expensive laboratories and equipment.

In another two years, more funds were available because the institution was completely transferred to the state. It was renamed Ngee Ann Technical College, and it was moved into a new campus at Clementi.[241]

Two more years went by. In 1970, it replaced its four-year Business Administration degree with a three-year diploma program.

Eight years after its founding and one year after downgrading to college status, in 1971, the college changed its medium of instruction from Mandarin to English.[242]

Even the second oldest institution of higher learning in Hong Kong was forced to give in. Despite keeping the word "Chinese" in its name, it is now teaching mostly in English[243].

Without the help of hindsight, Nanyang University was unable to interpret the writing on the wall. Because its faculty was overwhelmingly Chinese in orientation, and because some of its students and alumni protested the change, the attempt to transform itself into a bilingual institution was half-hearted and unsuccessful.

The prime minister, however, could not accept the prospect of several hundred students wasting their future, year after year, by entering the Chinese university and struggling to find jobs after graduation. Eleven Nantah-graduated ministers and members of Parliament agreed that he should intervened for the "greater good."[244] (S.O.S. – save our school.)

Some English-educated ministers were more judicious and less intrepid. They felt intervention was politically costly, and they were apprehensive about repercussions from donors and supporters of the university. The health minister and the environment minister were dead set against it. The deputy prime minister and the chairman of the Public Utilities Board were also not in favor. Even the labor minister, who was educated in a Chinese school but graduated from the English-medium university, had reservations. All of them preferred leaving it alone to die a natural death.[245] (It ain't worth the risk.)

The prime minister was favorably circumstanced in 1978, because the People's Action Party (PAP) not only won every general election for nineteen years, but secured every parliamentary seat for twelve years. He was also strengthened by the buoyant economy, with annual

GDP growth rates of 8.4% (1976), 7.8% (1977), 8.6% (1978)[246], enabling him to boldly go where his predecessors (and successors) feared to tread.

To raise the English competence of students in Nanyang University, he relocated that year's enrollment into the University of Singapore for English-language immersion. Under the Joint Campus Scheme, first-year students from both universities studied together in the same class. Nantah students found it difficult to adjust, while the English-stream students complained the former hampered their progress.[247]

Nantah students from the joint campus were asked, before they graduated, if they preferred a degree from the University of Singapore, or a degree from Nanyang University, or one that was jointly awarded by both universities. Most picked the first. And the government affirmed their choice by merging both universities in 1980, forming the National University of Singapore (NUS).[248]

The Chinese-educated community, who struggled to safeguard Chinese education since colonial times, believed these events revealed a plot to shut down or anglicize the Chinese university. And so, despite converting some Chinese-medium schools into Special Assistance Plan (SAP) schools, despite imposing second-language requirements for entry into junior colleges, as well as universities, despite streaming primary-school pupils on language ability, the chain revision of education policy hardly ameliorated their furious reaction, yet sent others scurrying abroad for refuge. (see Fig 9) The fallout disadvantaged still others. Boys, mostly.

Chapter 8

• • • • • • • • • •

THINKER BELLES
And the never-planned lost boys

The deputy prime minister-cum-education minister, in his speech at the 1980 Pre-U Seminar[250], said the number of twelfth-grade boys from all language streams taking the A-level examination that year was 2,816 out of 28,449 boys from the 1969 primary-one class. Girls numbered 3,908 out of 26,388. His figures worked out to just ten percent of boys, but fifteen percent of girls, finishing high school.

Students making the grade at A-levels were admitted into the newly merged university in 1981. Because girls enrolled right after admission, and boys enrolled two years later in June 1983, conscription obfuscated the quandary.

Two months after the boys enrolled into university, in August, the prime minister encouraged Singapore men to choose highly educated women as wives, sparking the Great Marriage Debate.

Five months later, despite the unfavorable public response to the prime minister's National Day Address, the government formed a match-making agency in January 1984. The agency helped university graduates – particularly female graduates – find lifelong partners.

Two months passed by. In March, the prime minister introduced natalist policies favoring graduate mothers. He proposed offering tax incentives, as well as placing their children more favorably in primary school registration. Women with less than ten years of education or earning less than $1,500 monthly were to be given cash incentives for sterilization and subject to punitive delivery fees.[251]

Both measures were unpopular:

- *The Social Development Unit (SDU).* It elicited derision and earned Singapore a reputation as the epitome of the nanny state.[252]
- *The Graduate Mothers' Scheme.* Nine months after it was announced in the nanny state, voters, who were gestated with indignation, delivered two parliamentary seats for the opposition, forcing the ill-conceived scheme to be later aborted.

Although the People's Action Party won a resounding victory at the general elections of December 1984, being returned to government with an overwhelming majority, they lost another constituency. This time because of protest votes.

(The incumbent party had won in every electoral district from 1968, but lost their first parliamentary seat in the 1981 by-election. That was one year after Nanyang University was closed, but it was not the main reason for their defeat.)

Their share of the vote, 65%, was also the lowest in twenty-one years, and the decrease was their largest at general elections, falling 13% from 78% share four years earlier.

A few months after the sixth parliamentary term opened, the newly appointed education minister in the revamped cabinet, Tony Tan, recommended discontinuing the pro-natal policies. The scheme to engender smarter babies was abandoned. But the gender disparity didn't go away.

Months passed.

Lee Kuan-yew suggested reinstating polygamy, civil unions that he had abolished after he became the prime minister in 1959.

Was he reviving the practice of taking concubines and harboring xùbì? Was he becoming obsessive with eugenics? Was he starting a public brainstorm with students, seeking out socially acceptable ways to resolve the gender imbalance? Whatever the reason may be, his speech at the National University of Singapore in 1986 triggered only a fusillade of criticism, to which he responded with reticence.

Only 10 out of every 100 boys, but 15 out of every 100 girls, sat for the A-level examination in 1980.

Chapter 9

● ● ● ● ● ● ● ● ● ●

SUCCESS
Only a work in progress

The removal of double weighting on languages at PSLE in 1985, marked the start of a series of changing emphasis. Mathematical standards were raised and second-language requirements eased for most students. And in this way, the education ministry forestalled the problem of having shelf after shelf after shelf of graduating spinsters.

Nowadays, testing third-graders in primary three for the *Gifted Education Program (GEP)* comprises only mathematics, English, and visual-spatial abilities. Mathematical Olympiads are also organized, letting popular middle and high schools admit contest winners and finalists. These students are admitted before they sit for national examinations. Boys, especially, prefer mathematics competition to spelling bees or moxiebisai, a Chinese-language recitation and dictation competition.

To help students who face exceptional difficulties with learning the language, the education ministry introduced the Chinese B syllabus at the middle and high schools.[253] It is also easier to get quality passes for Chinese language than English, Math, or Science at the sixth-grade national examination, or PSLE. (see below table)

National Standard PSLE Results Percentage for Quality Passes (A* & A)			
Subject	2010[254]	2011[255]	2012[256]
Chinese	81.2%	80.6%	80.7%
English	44.3%	44.3%	44.7%
Math	43.3%	43.5%	44.5%
Science	43.2%	43.5%	42.4%

Three top secondary schools for boys also offer alternative curricula that meet the educational needs of bright students who are not coping with the second language. The three international schools[257] were started between 2005 and 2006. They are coeducational, admitting female students because no girls' school has a similar program.

Nevertheless, linguistically inclined students in Singapore are encouraged to take Higher Chinese, an elective offered between primary five (fifth-graders) and secondary four (tenth-graders).[258] Outstanding students are offered bicultural studies scholarships[259] between second-ary three (ninth-graders) and junior college two (twelfth-graders), and some of these students may even receive scholarships to study at top universities in China.

At last, colonialism is banished. Communism is dead. Chinese chauvinism is buried. Not only were damsels rescued from the distressing incompetence of their hope-less suitors but Chinese-language teachers now skip into the sunset, content to know that their students are en-gaged in learning their "mother tongue."

The End?

Because schools now teach ahead to meet the needs of exceptionally able pupils, neither the boys nor the girls are living happily ever after. Children are frazzled, with academic redshirting denied to all but foreign students, and their parents help them cope by spending billions on afterschool tutoring. But that's … another story.

● ● ● ● ● ● ● ● ● ●

AMEN
An epilog on growth and advancement

Although he couldn't make Singapore a nation of linguistic geniuses, Lee Kuan-yew managed to carry out another scheme with less grandeur than eugenics. The more attainable policy aimed to create a Mandarin-speaking environment for students to reinforce language learning.

Lee started his crusade to make Mandarin popular in a television broadcast delivered on April 6, 1978. In *Bilingualism – A discussion with the Prime Minister*, he expressed his hope to get Mandarin spoken at the shops, on the busses, at the cinemas, and at the hawker centers. Launched by *The Promote Mandarin Council* on September 7, 1979, the *Speak Mandarin Campaign* encourages Chinese Singaporeans to use Mandarin. Its first goal was to stop all young Chinese from speaking other Sinitic languages in five years, and then usher in Mandarin as the language of choice in public places within ten years.[260] When the campaign was in its fifteenth year, the Singapore Chinese Chamber of Commerce abolished its bāng system, an electoral system based on clan divisions.

The philanthropist who founded Chinese High School and Xiamen University was formerly a president of the Singapore Chinese Chamber of Commerce. In 1927, he tried to get rid of the bāng-based voting process in the chamber, but his efforts were blocked because the non-Fúlǎo felt smaller clans would be disadvantaged. Voters, at that time, backed only their clansmen who were speaking their dialect. The community leader was an advocate for using Mandarin in Chinese education, even though he was unable to speak the language[261].

Other prominent leaders were also unsuccessful in getting members to rise above clan politics. As late as the nineteen-fifties and nineteen-sixties, impassioned clashes between members ensued whenever the issue was brought up during meetings.[262]

But by 1993, more Singaporeans were using Mandarin in place of other Sinitic languages, and that probably made it easier for a youthful forty-year-old president[263] of the chamber to end the clan-based method of elections. Reforming the Chinese Chamber of Commerce and making it more professional was, in turn, some years ahead of the increasing use of Mandarin in Shanghai.

Putonghua was extensively promoted in that city with public campaigns. The State Council of the People's Republic of China launched the campaign, *Popularize*

Putonghua, during the nineteen-fifties. But most were unable to understand Mandarin, let alone speak it, and elderly schoolteachers (and even some national leaders) were speaking incomprehensible Mandarin.[264]

The State Council conducted a second campaign in the nineteen-eighties. Shanghai Television also ran a Putonghua competition series, *I Love the Beautiful Language of the Fatherland*. Many people took part in the competition, but the use of Mandarin did not permeate the wider population. The Shanghainese people were not using Mandarin because it made them appear supercilious to their fellow urbanites.[265]

But globalization in the twenty-first century encouraged the use of Mandarin in Shanghai. Young people, who see no value in Shanghainese, are giving it up, and their elderly relatives accommodate them by speaking pidgin Mandarin.[266]

These days in Shanghai, students speak impeccable Mandarin. And indeed on several national Putonghua competency examinations, their teachers outperformed those from Beijing and other Mandarin-speaking cities. Most natives of the city routinely use Mandarin at the office, even though some outsiders may choose to speak Shanghainese, a situation that seems to be lau-kuah-sae-ngah, the local expression for weird.

But, in spite of their accomplishments, Mandarin is spoken at the shops, on the busses, at the cinemas, and at the hawker centers more in Singapore than in Shanghai. For today. As for tomorrow, I hope we stay ahead.

###

● ● ● ● ● ● ● ● ● ●

EXPLANATORY NOTES
And a list of references

1. For example, Alexander Pope rhymed "tea" with "obey" in his 1714 poem, The Rape of the Lock.

2. 钱生可。上海黑幕汇编 (Compilation of Shanghai's dark secrets). Shanghai, 1917, quoted in Goodman, Bryna, *Native Place, City, and Nation Regional Networks and Identities in Shanghai, 1853-1937*, Berkeley: University of California Press, 1995. In the first chapter, "Introduction: The Moral Excellence of Loving the Group", Bryna listed prostitutes from Suzhou, Ningbo, and Guangdong.

3. The League of Nations, CETWCE, p.95, quoted in Warren, J. F. *Ah Ku and Karayuki-san: Prostitution in Singapore, 1870 - 1940*. NUS Press, 2003. In "Chapter 4: Human Traffic and Brothel Prostitution", Warren gives an account of sex trafficking between Xiamen, Shantou, Shanghai. Guangzhou, Hong Kong, and Macau. The last two ports were key places of transit for traffic to Singapore.

4. Enclosure in No. 227 Acting Governor Sir J. H. Swenttenham to Mr Chamberlain, 5 August 1898, CO 882/6, quoted in Warren,

James Francis "Chapter 10: The Puller and the Public" In *Rickshaw Coolie: A People's History of Singapore, 1880-1940*. Singapore: Singapore University Press, 2003.

5. Yeoh, Brenda S. A. *Contesting Space: Power Relations and the Urban Built Environment in Colonial Singapore*. Kuala Lumpur: Oxford University Press, 1996. In "Appendix Table A.1.", the Singapore's Chinese population was reported to be 86,766 in 1881; 121,908 in 1891; 164,041 in 1901; and 164,041 in 1911. Using cubic spline interpolation, a population of 150,285 is calculated for the year 1898.

6. 李永球《太平开辟期的会党与华人籍贯探讨》人文杂志第十四期, March 3, 2002.

7. Ibid.

8. Ibid.

9. Ibid.

10. Ibid. Ngah Ibrahim captured and executed So Ah-chiang at Teluk Kertang. So was the leader of the Yìxīng Company.

11. Ibid. Hé Yìshòu founded the Héhé Society. Lǐ Yàkūn was the first faction chief. Chin Ah-yam was the second faction chief.

12. Ibid.

13. Ibid.

14. Overseas Chinese in the British Empire: Larut Wars." Accessed January 17, 2015. http://overseaschineseinthebritishempire.blogspot.sg/search/label/Larut Wars.

15. 李永球《太平开辟期的会党与华人籍贯探讨》人文杂志第十四期, March 3, 2002.

16. The leaders of the Yìxīng Company appealed for help. And because they were British subjects, the Straits Settlements Government responded.

17. Ho, Engseng. *Gangsters Into Gentlemen: The Breakup of Multiethnic Conglomerates and The Rise of A Straits Chinese Identity in Penang*. Penang Heritage Trust & STAR Publications, 2002.

18. Leung, Yuen-sang, "The economic life of the Chinese in late nineteenth-century Singapore", in Lee, Lai To. *Early Chinese Immigrant Societies: Case Studies from North America and British Southeast Asia*. Singapore: Heinemann Asia, 1988.

19. Lee, Edwin "Chapter 6: The Protector of Chinese" In *The British as Rulers: Governing Multiracial Singapore, 1867-1914*. Singapore: Singapore University Press, National University of Singapore, 1991.

20. Yong, C. F., and R. B. McKenna. *The Kuomintang Movement in British Malaya, 1912-1949*. Singapore: Singapore University Press, National University of Singapore, 1990.

21. "WHY EMPLOY HYLAMS?" The Straits Times, September 29, 1928, quoted in Kenley, David L. *New Culture in a New World: The May Fourth Movement and the Chinese Diaspora in Singapore, 1919-1932*. New York: Routledge, 2003.

22. Saw, Swee-hock. *The Population of Singapore*. 3rd ed. Singapore: Institute of Southeast Asian Studies, 2012.

23. 《新加坡華人》 - 维基百科，自由的百科全书. Accessed January 17, 2015.

24. 林旭娜、通讯员、沈卫红与黄爱华 《三水红头巾 挑起新加坡》南方日报, June 8, 2011.

25. 《新加坡華人》 – 维基百科，自由的百科全书. Accessed January 17, 2015.

26. Chin, Peng, and Ian Ward. *My Side of History*. Singapore: Media Masters, 2003.

27. Blythe, Wilfred. *The Impact of Chinese Secret Societes in Malaya: A Historical Study*. London: Oxford University Press, 1969, quoted in Trocki, Carl A. *Opium and Empire: Chinese Society in Colonial Singapore, 1800-1910*. Ithaca, N.Y.: Cornell University Press, 1990.

28. Wyunhe "File:Map of Sinitic Dialect - English Version.svg" - Wikimedia Commons. May 10, 2011. Accessed January 16, 2015.

29. 《普通话》 百度百科 – 互动百科. Accessed January 21, 2015. http://www.baike.com/wiki/普通话.

30. Moszczynski "File:Madarin in Chinese Mainland EN.PNG" Wikimedia Commons. June 22, 2012. Accessed January 16, 2015.

31. For example, Begbie regarded the Teochew Chinese as Cantonese.
    Begbie, P. J. *The Malayan Peninsula*. Kuala Lumpur: Oxford University Press, 1967, quoted in Trocki, Carl A. *Prince of Pirates: The Temenggongs and the Development of Johor and Singapore, 1784-1885*. 2nd ed. Singapore: NUS Press, 2007.

32. "Yue Chinese" Wikipedia. Accessed January 21, 2015. http://en.wikipedia.org/wiki/Yue_Chinese.

33. "Yuehai Dialects" Wikipedia. Accessed January 21, 2015. http://en.wikipedia.org/wiki/Yuehai_dialects.

34. Ibid.

35. 《标准粤语编辑》标准粤语_百度百科. Accessed January 21, 2015. http://baike.baidu.com/view/7064658.htm.

36. Base Map drawn by ASDFGH, and it is on display at En.wikipedia "File:Yue Dialects.png" Wikimedia Commons. October 31, 2008. Accessed January 16, 2015.

37. 李永球《太平开辟期的会党与华人籍贯探讨》人文杂志第十四期, March 3, 2002.

38. Ibid.

39. Base Map modified from http://www.cinarc.org/Regions.html. October 31, 2008. Accessed August 17, 2015.

40. 李永球《太平开辟期的会党与华人籍贯探讨》人文杂志第十四期, March 3, 2002.

41. Trocki, Carl A. Singapore *Wealth, Power and the Culture of Control*. London: Routledge, 2006. Trocki uses the Mǐnnán pronunciation: "Quan Teck (or Kien Teck) Hui." I assume the society had the same name as Jiàndé (Kian Tek) Huì at Penang.

42. Trocki, Carl A. *Opium, Empire, and the Global Political Economy: A Study of the Asian Opium Trade, 1750-1950*. London: Routledge, 1999.

43. Ibid.

44. 王琛发《异乡开埠：清代客家矿商在马来亚的成与败》孝恩杂志, March 15, 2013.

45. Ibid.

46. Trocki, Carl A. *Singapore Wealth, Power and the Culture of Control*. London: Routledge, 2006.

47. 王琛发 《异乡开埠：清代客家矿商在马来亚的成与败》孝恩杂志, March 15, 2013.

48. Ibid.

49. Ibid.

50. Ibid.

51. Ibid.

52. Ibid.

53. 《莆田话编辑》莆田话_百度百科. Accessed January 21, 2015. http://baike.baidu.com/view/909013.htm.

54. 《闽东语编辑》闽东语_百度百科. Accessed January 21, 2015. http://baike.baidu.com/view/1256763.htm

55. 《福佬民系编辑》福佬民系_百度百科. Accessed January 21, 2015. http://baike.baidu.com/view/1551253.htm.

56. 《泉州话 锁定 编辑》泉州话_百度百科. Accessed January 21, 2015. http://baike.baidu.com/view/399388.htm.

57. 《漳州话编辑》漳州话_百度百科. Accessed January 21, 2015. http://baike.baidu.com/view/1739213.htm.

58. Turnbull, Mary "Penang's Changing Role in the Straits Settlements, 1826-1946" *The Penang Story – International Conference 2002*, April 18, 2002.

59. Liu, Hong, and Wong, Sin-kiong. *Singapore Chinese Society in Transition: Business, Politics, & Socio-economic Change, 1945-1965*. New York: Peter Lang, 2004.

60. Ibid.

61. Trocki, Carl A. *Opium, Empire, and the Global Political Economy: A Study of the Asian Opium Trade, 1750-1950*. London: Routledge, 1999. The Jiàndé Society made its appearance in Singapore around the 1846 riots.

62. 《潮州话编辑》潮州话_百度百科. Accessed January 21, 2015. http://baike.baidu.com/view/39085.htm.

63. 谭铮、林丽丽与何满洪 《广东汕头澄海樟林古港:昔日古港今民居(高清组图)》 中国日报网, December 11, 2014.

64. 《潮州话编辑》潮州话_百度百科. Accessed January 21, 2015. http://baike.baidu.com/view/39085.htm.

65. Warren, James Francis. *Rickshaw Coolie: A People's History of Singapore, 1880-1940*. Singapore: Singapore University Press, 2003.

66. Ah-Q is a fictional character in *The True Story of Ah Q*, a novella written by Lu Xun.

67. Warren, James Francis. *Rickshaw Coolie: A People's History of Singapore, 1880-1940*. Singapore: Singapore University Press, 2003.

68. Ibid.

69. Ibid.

70. Ibid.

71. Ibid.

72. Ibid.

73. Thulaja, Naidu Ratnala "Duxton Road" Singapore Infopedia. Accessed January 22, 2015. http://eresources.nlb.gov.sg/infopedia/articles/SIP_357_2005-01-22.html.

74. Chin, Peng, and Ian Ward. *My Side of History*. Singapore: Media Masters, 2003.

75. Visscher, Sikko. *The Business of Politics and Ethnicity: A History of the Singapore Chinese Chamber of Commerce and Industry*. Singapore: NUS Press, 2007.

76. "Xuan Wu (god)" Wikipedia. Accessed January 23, 2015. http://en.wikipedia.org/wiki/Xuan_Wu_(god).

77. Khoo, Salma Nasution. *Streets of George Town, Penang*. 4th ed. Penang, Malaysia: Areca Books, 2007. She wrote that during the nineteenth-century, every Chinese craftsman and builder would first call at the Lo Pan Temple in Penang.

78. Cheang Hong-lim was the leader of the Changtai bāng.

79. Rev Ling Ching-mi was the pastor from Fuzhou. Rev Lau Seng-chong was the Mǐnnán-speaking pastor.

80. Shen, Lingxie "The Sanjiangren in Singapore" *Chinese Southern Diaspora Studies 5*, no. 2011-12 (2012). http://chl.anu.edu.au/sites/csds/.

81. "Wu Chinese: Names" Wikipedia. Accessed January 17, 2015. http://en.wikipedia.org/wiki/Wu_Chinese#Names.

82. Shen, Lingxie "The Sanjiangren in Singapore" *Chinese Southern Diaspora Studies 5*, no. 2011-12 (2012). http://chl.anu.edu.au/sites/csds/.

83. Ibid.

84. Ibid.

85. Ibid.

86. "About Us" Singapore Sam Kiang Huay Kwan. Accessed January 17, 2015. http://www.samkiang.org/?page_id=368.

87. For example, past statistical records of the Singapore Chinese Chamber of Commerce used Sanjiang and Shanghainese synonymously. Some of these statistics are quoted in Visscher, Sikko. *The Business of Politics and Ethnicity: A History of the Singapore Chinese Chamber of Commerce and Industry*. Singapore: NUS Press, 2007.
Incidentally, Singapore's Indian immigrants, who were mostly from Tamil Nadu, used to regard all arrivals from northern India as Bengali people, even if the latter were neither from Bengal region nor able to speak Bengali.

88. "About Us" Singapore Sam Kiang Huay Kwan. Accessed January 17, 2015. http://www.samkiang.org/?page_id=368.

89. Saw, Swee-hock. The Population of Singapore. 3rd ed. Singapore: Institute of Southeast Asian Studies, 2012.

90. Ibid.

91. Buckley, Charles Burton. *An anecdotal history of old times in Singapore 1819-1867*. Singapore: Oxford University Press, 1984.

92. Wilson, Harold E. *Social Engineering in Singapore: Educational Policies and Social Change, 1819-1972*. Singapore: Singapore University Press, 1978.

93. Buckley, Charles Burton. *An anecdotal history of old times in Singapore 1819-1867*. Singapore: Oxford University Press, 1984.

94. "The SJI Milestones" Saint Joseph's Institution. http://www.sji.edu.sg/about-sji/the-sji-milestones.

95. "St Andrew's School is established" HistorySG. http://ere-sources.nlb.gov.sg/history/events/7fb18ee7-0029-4e73-9296-b78f1fde5033.
96. "Saint Andrew's School, Singapore" Wikipedia. Accessed January 16, 2015. http://en.wikipedia.org/wiki/Saint_Andrew's_School,_Singapore.
    Sim Quee and Tye Kim were the Chinese owners.
97. Cheang Hong-lim was the leader of the Changtai bāng. He had paid for the repair and improvement of Fúdé Temple in 1869, and he was also notable in other charitable giving.
98. Chop is a colloquial name for a Chinese seal, usually made of stone. The seal would be imprinted in Chinese characters the name of an individual, his office, or his business. Using the seal to stamp documents and contracts with red ink would prove the identity of the party bound to the agreement, akin to signatures used by the colonizers. Since businesses and companies were not registered, the name on these seals also served as business names.
99. Savage, Victor R., and Brenda S. A. Yeoh. *Singapore Street Names a Study of Toponymics.* Singapore: Marshall Cavendish, 2013.
100. Cheang Jim Hean Free School was named after Cheang Jim-hean, the eldest son of Cheang Hong-lim.
101. Song, Ong-siang. One Hundred Years' History of the Chinese in Singapore, quoted in "9 Generations down the Road to Hong Lim Park" - Bukit Brown Cemetery : Our Roots, Our Future. Accessed January 23, 2015. http://blog.bukit-brown.org/post/44373409996/9-generations-down-the-road-to-hong-lim-park.
102. "History" St. Anthony's Primary School. Accessed January 16, 2015. http://www.stanthonyspri.moe.edu.sg/our-school/history.
103. "Gan Eng Seng" Wikipedia. Accessed June 21, 2016. https://en.wikipedia.org/wiki/Gan_Eng_Seng.
104. "GESS History" Gan Eng Seng School. Accessed January 16, 2015. http://www.ganengsengsch.moe.edu.sg/about-us/history/gess-history/.

105. "Anglo-Chinese School" Wikipedia. Accessed January 16, 2015. http://en.wikipedia.org/wiki/Anglo-Chinese_School.

106. "Singapore Chinese Girls' School" Wikipedia. Accessed January 16, 2015. http://en.wikipedia.org/wiki/Singapore_Chinese_Girls"_School.

107. "Song Ong Siang" Wikipedia. Accessed January 18, 2015. http://en.wikipedia.org/wiki/Song_Ong_Siang.

108. "Victoria School" Wikipedia. Accessed January 20, 2015. http://en.wikipedia.org/wiki/Victoria_School#History.

109. Wilson, Harold E. *Social Engineering in Singapore: Educational Policies and Social Change, 1819-1972*. Singapore: Singapore University Press, 1978.

110. The Ten-year Plan. (1947)

111. "Maria Dyer" Singapore Infopedia. http://eresources.nlb.gov.sg/infopedia/articles/SIP_1343_2008-12-10.html.

112. Chng, David K Y 《崇文阁等（四）》卡萨布兰卡 http://cocoissey.blog.sohu.com/67054528.html. The leader of the Fúlǎo community, Tan Kim-seng, and the founder of the Cháoshàn foundation, Seah Eu-chin, sponsored the building of the Chóngwén Gé.

113. "13. Chwee Eng Chinese School, 1854, Conserved" Historic Chinese Architecture in Singapore. August 6, 2005. Accessed January 16, 2015. https://nanyangtemple.wordpress.com/2005/08/07/13-chwee-eng-chinese-school-1854-conserved/.

114. Vaughan, J. D. *Manners and Customs of the Chinese in the Straits Settlements*. Singapore: Mission Press, 1879, quoted in Trocki, Carl A. Opium and Empire: Chinese Society in Colonial Singapore, 1800-1910. Ithaca, N.Y.: Cornell University Press, 1990.

115. "Our History" Holy Innocents High School. Accessed January 16, 2015. http://www.holyinnocentshigh.moe.edu.sg/our-hihs/our-history/.

116. Lee, Ting-hui. *Chinese Schools in British Malaya: Policies and Politics*. Singapore: South Seas Society, 2006.

117. Ibid.

118. "GESS History" Gan Eng Seng School. Accessed January 16, 2015. http://www.ganengsengsch.moe.edu.sg/about-us/history/gess-history/.

119. Lim, Siew-yeen, and Renuka M. "Tao Nan School" Singapore Infopedia. Accessed January 23, 2015. http://eresources.nlb.gov.sg/infopedia/articles/SIP_608_2005-01-04.html.

120. Ibid.

121. Ibid.

122. "Women and Confucianism" Women in World History Curriculum. Accessed January 23, 2015. http://www.womeninworldhistory.com/lesson3.html.

123. "New Culture Movement" Wikipedia. Accessed January 23, 2015. http://en.wikipedia.org/wiki/New_Culture_Movement.

124. "Work Keeps Them from Running Wild" *The Singapore Free Press.* 7 July 1954, Page 5.

125. Lee, Ting-hui. *Chinese Schools in British Malaya: Policies and Politics.* Singapore: South Seas Society, 2006.

126. Yong, C. F., and R. B. McKenna. *The Kuomintang Movement in British Malaya, 1912-1949.* Singapore: Singapore University Press, National University of Singapore, 1990.

127. "Sun Yat-sen" Wikipedia. Accessed January 23, 2015. http://en.wikipedia.org/wiki/Sun_Yat-sen.

128. Lee, Ting-hui. *Chinese Schools in British Malaya: Policies and Politics.* Singapore: South Seas Society, 2006.

129. The colonial secretary, Andrew Caldecott, in his reply to demands for more education in English. Quoted in Pennycook, Alastair. *The Cultural Politics of English as an International Language.* London: Longman, 1994.

130. The governor, Cecil Clementi, in his lengthy defense following Caldecott's speech. Quoted in Pennycook, Alastair. *The Cultural Politics of English as an International Language.* London: Longman, 1994.

131. The Income Tax Ordinance was enacted only in 1947.

132. Lee, Ting-hui. *Chinese Schools in British Malaya: Policies and Politics.* Singapore: South Seas Society, 2006.

133. Kuo, H. Y. "Rescuing Businesses through Transnationalism: Embedded Chinese Enterprise and Nationalist Activities in Singapore in the 1930s Great Depression" *Enterprise and Society*, 2006, 98-127.

134. Lee, Ting-hui. *Chinese Schools in British Malaya: Policies and Politics*. Singapore: South Seas Society, 2006.

135. Ibid.

136. Ibid.

137. Ibid.

138. Ibid.

139. Ibid.

140. Ibid.

141. Ibid.
    (Lok Khwan Night School, Lok lok, and Ng lok were Hainanese schools.)

142. Ibid.

143. Ibid.

144. Ibid.

145. Ibid.

146. Warren, James Francis. *Rickshaw Coolie: A People's History of Singapore, 1880-1940*. Singapore: Singapore University Press, 2003. Warren noted incidents where corpses were abandoned beside a road, dumped into the Kallang River, and left on someone's verandah. Some people who were terminally ill were also abandoned.

147. Saw, Swee-hock. *The Population of Singapore*. 3rd ed. Singapore: Institute of Southeast Asian Studies, 2012.

148. Saw, Swee-hock. *The Population of Peninsular Malaysia*. Singapore: Institute of Southeast Asian Studies, 2007.

149. Lee Kuan-yew estimated the death toll from 50,000 to 100,000 young men in a Discovery Channel programme. https://www.youtube.com/watch?v=MQvvNdxSTgw, quoted in "Sook Ching" Wikipedia. Accessed January 20, 2015.

150. Saw, Swee-hock. *The Population of Singapore*. 3rd ed. Singapore: Institute of Southeast Asian Studies, 2012.

151. Turnbull, C. M. *A History of Modern Singapore, 1819-2005*. Singapore: NUS Press, 2009. Tan Kah-kee was refused entry.
152. Chin, Peng, and Ian Ward. *My Side of History*. Singapore: Media Masters, 2003.
153. Saw, Swee-hock. *The Population of Singapore*. 3rd ed. Singapore: Institute of Southeast Asian Studies, 2012.
154. Wilson, Harold E. *Social Engineering in Singapore: Educational Policies and Social Change, 1819-1972*. Singapore: Singapore University Press, 1978.
155. Ibid.
156. Ibid.
157. "Japanese Occupation of Singapore." Wikipedia. Accessed January 28, 2015. http://en.wikipedia.org/wiki/Japanese_occupation_of_Singapore.
158. Wong, Ting-hong. *Hegemonies Compared: State Formation and Chinese School Politics in Postwar Singapore and Hong Kong*. New York: RoutledgeFalmer, 2002.
159. Loh Kok Wah, "From tin mine coolies to agricultural squatters: socio—economic change in the Kinta District during the inter-war years", in P. J. Rimmer and L. Allen. *The Underside of Malaysian History: Pullers, Prostitutes, Plantation Workers*. Singapore: Singapore University Press for Malaysia Society of the Asian Studies Association of Australia, 1990.
160. Saw, Swee-hock. *The Population of Singapore*. 3rd ed. Singapore: Institute of Southeast Asian Studies, 2012.
161. Ibid.
162. (i)The Immigration Ordinance (No. 5), 1952. (ii)Immigration Regulations, 1953. (iii)Immigration (Prohibition Entry) Order, 1953.
163. Low, Kelvin E. Y. *Remembering the Samsui Women: Migration and Social Memory in Singapore and China*. Vancouver: UBC Press, 2014.
164. Department of Social Welfare, A social survey of Singapore (Singapore, 1947), quoted in Turnbull, C. M. *A History of Modern Singapore, 1819-2005*. Singapore: NUS Press, 2009.

165. Wilson, Harold E. *Social Engineering in Singapore*: Educational Policies and Social Change, 1819-1972. Singapore: Singapore University Press, 1978.

166. According to the 1947 census, literacy rate was 374 per thousand. Quoted in Del Tufo, M. V. (1949). *Malaya, comprising the Federation of Malaya and the colony of Singapore: A report on the 1947 census of population*, quoted in "Singapore's First Postwar Census." Singapore Infopedia. Accessed January 28, 2015. http://eresources.nlb.gov.sg/infopedia/articles/SIP_2014-06-16_150036.html.

167. Wilson, Harold E. *Social Engineering in Singapore: Educational Policies and Social Change, 1819-1972*. Singapore: Singapore University Press, 1978.

168. Ibid.

169. Ibid.

170. Ibid.

171. Ibid.

172. Ibid.

173. Ibid.

174. Ibid.

175. Ibid.

176. Ibid.

177. Ibid.

178. Ibid.

179. Wong, Ting-hong. *Hegemonies Compared: State Formation and Chinese School Politics in Postwar Singapore and Hong Kong*. New York: RoutledgeFalmer, 2002.

180. Wilson, Harold E. *Social Engineering in Singapore: Educational Policies and Social Change, 1819-1972*. Singapore: Singapore University Press, 1978.

181. Comber, Leon. *Singapore Correspondent: Political Dispatches from Singapore (1958-1962)*. Singapore: Marshall Cavendish Editions, 2012.

182. Ibid.

183. Ibid.

184. Ibid.

185. Ibid.

Lim Yew-hock was the chief minister.

Singapore's unemployment rate in 1958 was indeed high at 13%. But even though Australia faced the same unemployment rate in 1993, neither school leavers nor university graduates in Australia had to compete with 100-plus applicants for entry-level jobs.

186. Ibid.

Chew Swee-kee was the education minister.

187. Quoted in an address by the Prime Minister, Mr. Lee Kuan-yew, at the opening ceremony of the "Promote the Use of Mandarin" campaign on 7th September 1979.

188. Turnbull, C. M. *A History of Modern Singapore, 1819-2005*. Singapore: NUS Press, 2009.

189. "Queen's Scholar (British Malaya and Singapore)." Wikipedia. Accessed May 29, 2015. http://en.wikipedia.org/wiki/Queen%27s_Scholar_%28British_Malaya_and_Singapore%29.

190. Goh, Chor-boon. *Technology and Entrepôt Colonialism in Singapore, 1819-1940*. Institute of Southeast Asian Studies, 2013.

191. Guay Ee-ling, and Joanna HS Tan. "Raffles College." Singapore Infopedia. Accessed January 28, 2015. http://eresources.nlb.gov.sg/infopedia/articles/SIP_1797_2011-03-15.html.

192. Wilson, Harold E. *Social Engineering in Singapore: Educational Policies and Social Change, 1819-1972*. Singapore: Singapore University Press, 1978.

193. Ibid.

194. Ibid.

195. Ibid.

196. Mason, Frederic. *The Schools of Malaya*. 3th ed. Singapore: D. Moore, 1959.

197. Wilson, Harold E. *Social Engineering in Singapore: Educational Policies and Social Change, 1819-1972*. Singapore: Singapore University Press, 1978.

198. Ibid.

199. Ibid.

200. Ibid.

201. "COLONY'S AIM IS ALSO ONE SCHOOL FOR ALL, SAYS MR. FRISBY." The Straits Times, June 12, 1951, quoted in Wilson, Harold E. *Social Engineering in Singapore: Educational Policies and Social Change, 1819-1972.* Singapore: Singapore University Press, 1978.

202. "Historical Atlas of the British Empire" Accessed January 28, 2015. http://www.atlasofbritempire.com/uploads/1939_British_Diaspora.gif.

203. "Sihai Huayi Zongtu." Wikipedia. Accessed January 28, 2015. http://en.wikipedia.org/wiki/Sihai_Huayi_Zongtu.

204. On the map of "the British Empire British Diaspora", Malaya is the lower part of the peninsula at the southernmost point of the Asian mainland. Situated at the tip of Malaya is a little red dot, marked "Singapore." (Please zoom in to magnify the area if the dot is not visible on your screen.)

205. Wilson, Harold E. *Social Engineering in Singapore: Educational Policies and Social Change, 1819-1972.* Singapore: Singapore University Press, 1978

206. Saw, Swee-hock. *The Population of Peninsular Malaysia.* Singapore: Institute of Southeast Asian Studies, 2007.

207. Eight detainees were released: Devan Nair, Lim Chin-siong, Fong Swee-suan, Sidney Woodhull, James Puthucheary, Tan Chong-king, Chan Say-jame, and Chan Chiew-thor.

208. Lee, Edwin. *Singapore the Unexpected Nation.* Singapore: Institute of Southeast Asian Studies (ISEAS), 2008.

209. Lee, Kuan-yew. *My Lifelong Challenge: Singapore's Bilingual Journey.* Singapore: Straits Times Press, 2012.

210. Ibid.

211. Ibid.

212. Tan, Yap-kwang, Hong-kheng Chow, and Christine Goh. *Examinations in Singapore Change and Continuity (1891-2007) .* Singapore: World Scientific, 2008.

213. Ibid., percentage passes was 68%.

214. Ibid., percentage passes was 34%.

215. Chia Siew-hock. "An Investigation into Language Use Among Secondary Four Pupils in Singapore", 1977, quoted by Lim, Lisa, Anne Pakir, and Lionel Wee. *English in Singapore: Modernity and Management.* Singapore: Hong Kong University Press, 2010.

216. Krause, Lawrence B., and Ai Tee Koh. *The Singapore Economy Reconsidered.* Singapore: Institute of Southeast Asian Studies, 1987.

217. Lee, Sing. *Toward a Better Future Education and Training for Economic Development in Singapore since 1965.* Washington, D.C.: World Bank, 2008.

218. Lee, Edwin. *Singapore the Unexpected Nation.* Singapore: Institute of Southeast Asian Studies (ISEAS), 2008.

219. Lee, Kuan-yew. *My Lifelong Challenge: Singapore's Bilingual Journey.* Singapore: Straits Times Press, 2012.

220. Ibid.

221. Lee, Kuan-yew. *The Singapore Story.* Abridged Edition. Singapore: Times Media Private, 2000.

222. FO 371/14728/2082, Shorthand Report of a Conference at Government House, quoted by Yong, C. F., and R. B. McKenna. *The Kuomintang Movement in British Malaya, 1912-1949.* Singapore: Singapore University Press, National University of Singapore, 1990.

223. Lee, Edwin. *The British as Rulers: Governing Multiracial Singapore, 1867-1914.* Singapore: Singapore University Press, National University of Singapore, 1991.

224. Lee, Edwin. *Singapore the Unexpected Nation.* Singapore: Institute of Southeast Asian Studies (ISEAS), 2008.

225. "These BAs won't do says Chew." The Straits Times, 2 May 1956, Page 4, quoted in "Nanyang University." Singapore Infopedia. http://eresources.nlb.gov.sg/infopedia/articles/SIP_91_2005-02-02.html. Chew Swee-kee was the education minister.

226. Lee, Edwin. *Singapore the Unexpected Nation.* Singapore: Institute of Southeast Asian Studies (ISEAS), 2008.

227. Ibid.

228. Ibid.

229. Ibid.

230. Ibid.

231. Lee, Kuan-yew. *My Lifelong Challenge: Singapore's Bilingual Journey.* Singapore: Straits Times Press, 2012.

232. 马兴中. 《暨南大学与泰国》暨南新闻网. April 21, 2004. Accessed January 24, 2015. http://jnnews.jnu.edu.cn/html/2004/4/1293.htm.

233. 马兴中. 《暨南大学与印度尼西亚》暨南大学报, May 9, 2006. Accessed January 24, 2015. http://www.cunews.edu.cn/html2006/xbwc/143211146.html

234. Lee, Kuan-yew. *My Lifelong Challenge: Singapore's Bilingual Journey.* Singapore: Straits Times Press, 2012.

235. Ibid. Ong Pang-boon was the education minister.

236. Ibid.

237. Li, Xiaobing, and Hongshan Li. *China and the United States: A New Cold War History.* 1997.

238. Ma, Ai-hsuan Sandra. International Student Recruitment to Universities in Taiwan: Changing Discourses and Agendas. TASA Conference, 2010.

239. "Historical Milestones." Ngee Ann Polytechnic. Accessed January 30, 2015. http://www.np.edu.sg/home/aboutnp/history/Pages/con_history.aspx.

240. Ibid.

241. Ibid.

242. Ibid.

243. "CUHK Q&A section for mainland students." (8) 主修科多以英文授课, quoted in "Chinese University of Hong Kong." Wikipedia. Accessed January 30, 2015. http://en.wikipedia.org/wiki/Chinese University of Hong Kong.

244. Lee, Kuan-yew. *My Lifelong Challenge: Singapore's Bilingual Journey.* Singapore: Straits Times Press, 2012. Chai Chong-yii, Ch'ng Jit-koon, and Ho Kah-leong were among the eleven.

245. Ibid. Dr. Toh Chin-chye was the health minister. E.W. Barker was the environment minister. Dr. Goh Keng-swee was both

the deputy prime minister and the education minister. Lim Kim-san was the chairman of the Public Utilities Board. Ong Pang-boon was the labour minister.
246. Lee, Edwin. *Singapore the Unexpected Nation*. Singapore: Institute of Southeast Asian Studies (ISEAS), 2008.
247. Lee, Kuan-yew. *My Lifelong Challenge: Singapore's Bilingual Journey*. Singapore: Straits Times Press, 2012.
248. Ibid.
249. Immigrations graphs from the DIMA (Department of Immigration and Multicultural Affairs), quoted in Coughlan, James E., "The Changing Characteristics of Chinese Migrants to Australia During the 1980s and Early 1990s", in Sinn, Elizabeth. *The Last Half Century of Chinese Overseas*. Hong Kong: Hong Kong University Press, 1998.
250. Goh, Keng-swee, Speech at the Pre-U Seminar, "Partners in Progress with Trade Unions", June 1980, in Goh, Keng-swee, and Linda Low. *Wealth of East Asian Nations*. 2nd ed. Singapore: Marshall Cavendish Academic, 2004.
251. Trocki, Carl A. *Singapore Wealth, Power and the Culture of Control*. London: Routledge, 2006.
252. Buruma, Ian. *The Missionary and the Libertine: Love and War in East and West*. New York: Random House, 2000.
253. "Refinements to Mother Tongue Language Policy." Ministry of Education Singapore. Accessed January 31, 2015. http://www.moe.gov.sg/media/press/2004/pr20040109.htm.
254. "P4 Meet The Parents Session (5 March 2011)" Mee Toh School. Accessed January 31, 2015. http://www.meetoh.moe.edu.sg/wbn/slot/u1383/P4 Meet The Parents Session (5 March 2011).pdf
255. "RSS Link May 2012 Edition" Red Swastika School. Accessed January 31, 2015. http://www.redswastika.moe.edu.sg/wbn/slot/u2769/docs/RSS Link May 2012 Edition.pdf

256. "PSLE Performance 2012" Zhangde Primary School. Accessed January 31, 2015. http://www.zhang-depri.moe.edu.sg/pdf/achievements/PSLE/PSLE_Perfor-mance_2012.pdf

257. Anglo-Chinese School (International), Hwa Chong International School, St Joseph's Institution International School

258. "Refinements to Mother Tongue Language Policy." Ministry of Education Singapore. Accessed January 31, 2015. http://www.moe.gov.sg/media/press/2004/pr20040109.htm.

259. "Nurturing a Core of Students with Advanced Knowledge of Chinese Language and Culture." Ministry of Education Singapore. Accessed January 31, 2015. http://www.moe.gov.sg/media/press/2004/pr20040903.htm.

260. Lee, Kuan-yew. *My Lifelong Challenge: Singapore's Bilingual Journey.* Singapore: Straits Times Press, 2012.

261. C.F.Yong. *Tan Kah-kee: The Making of an Overseas Chinese Legend.* World Scientific, 2014. Tan Kah-kee relied on Lee Tiat-ming and others for Mandarin interpretation during his travels in China. Mr Lee was his personal secretary.

262. Visscher, Sikko. *The Business of Politics and Ethnicity: A History of the Singapore Chinese Chamber of Commerce and Industry.* Singapore: NUS Press, 2007.

263. The president, Kwek Leng-joo, was then forty years old.

264. 上海人学普通话. Documentary Film.

265. Ibid.

266. Xu, Junqian. "Shanghai Dialect Locked in Tug of War with Mandarin." *China Daily.*

###

GLOSSARY

Chinese Romanization 【Chinese Characters】 Notes

Ai Chun (Eastern-mǐn) Reading Room 【爱群书报社】 see Àiqún Reading Room

Ai Tong School 【爱同学校】 a primary school

Àiqún Reading Room 【爱群书报社】 a reading room

Amoy (Fúlǎo) 【厦门】 see Xiàmén

Ānxī Xiàn 【安溪县】 former Ānxī county in Quánzhōu prefecture. Now Ānxī city

Baba (Malay) 【-】 a term used by the Malays, referring to the Straits-Chinese men.

bak-gong (Yuèhǎi) 【北江】 Beijiang River in Guangdong Province

bāng 【帮】 group / gang / clique / party / secret society

bāngpài 【帮派】 gang / faction

bân-lâm (Fúlǎo) 【闽南】 see Mǐnnán

Barisan Sosialis (Malay) 【社会主义阵线】 Socialist Front, a left-wing political party formed in 1961.

bē-á (Fúlǎo) 【妹仔】 young girl.(see also mui tsai)

běndì 【本地】 local

bié-mǎ-tuǐ 【蹩马腿】 Hobble the horse's leg, a tactical move in Chinese chess.

Black Heavenly Emperor 【玄天上帝】 a daoist deity.

bo-vad-di (Hainanese) 【不识字】 illiterate

bo-vad-di (Hainanese) 【不识死】 act recklessly

Chang Chew hu (Fúlǎo) 【漳州府】 see Zhāngzhōu

Cháo'ān 【潮安】 a district in Chaozhou city, Guangdong Province.

Cháoshàn 【潮汕】 a dialect of Mǐnnán; the linguistic and cultural region in the east Guangdong, which is developing into a single metropolis.

Cháoyáng 【潮阳】 During Qing dynasty, a district in Chaozhou Prefecture, Guangdong Province

Chaozhou fǔ 【潮州府】 a former prefecture in Guangdong province.

Char Boh Kan (Fúlǎo) 【查某嫻】 This is the Penang Chinese pronunciation, probably based on the Zhangzhou dialect. It is pronounced as "Tsa Bóo Kán" in the Taiwanese language.

Cheang Jim Hean (Fúlǎo) Free School 【章芳林义校】 school started by Cheang Hong Lim and Cheang Jim Hean

Cheang Wan Seng (Fúlǎo) School 【章苑生学校】 school started by Cheang Hong Lim

Chih Tung (Kèjiā) Reading Room 【志同书报社】 see Zhìtóng Reading Room

Chin Chew hu (Fúlǎo) 【泉州府】 see Quánzhōu

Chin Kang Kuan (Fúlǎo) 【晋江县】 see Jìnjiāng Xiàn

Chóngwén Gé 【崇文阁】 Chóngwén Pavilion

Chui Eng (Fúlǎo) Institute 【萃英书院】 see Cuì yīng shū yuàn

Cuì yīng shū yuàn 【萃英书院】 first Chinese School in Singapore, founded in 1854.

dà-jiǎng-pǔtōnghuà-yùndòng 【大讲普通话运动】 a campaign in Shanghai to promote the use of Mandarin.

Dàbó Gōng 【大伯公】 Literal: "Grand Uncle." One of the pantheon of Malaysian Chinese Gods.

Dabu 【大埔】 During Qing dynasty, a county in Chaozhou Prefecture, Guangdong Province

Dào 【道】 Literal: "way". The Dào of Daoism is a philosophy and a religion.

dao-jiang-hu (Shanghainese) 【淘浆糊】 Literal: remove starch by washing rice before cooking. Metaphorical: full of crap.

dī-zú 【低卒】 In Chinese chess, refers to pawns that reached the opponent's throat rank

Duanmeng School 【端蒙学校】 Students and their parents in Singapore preferred English-medium schools. By the nineteen-nineties, the school was forced to close because there were not enough Chinese-stream students to con-tinue.

Eng Choon (Fúlǎo) 【永春】 see Yǒngchūn

Eng Teng (Kèjiā) 【永定】 See Yǒngdìng

ér huà 【儿化】 non-syllabic final r (儿) added to a word in spoken Chinese

Fǎ Zhǔgōng 【法主公】 lit. "Master of the Way", a Daoist deity

Fēngshùn 【丰顺】 Fengshun county in Meizhou, Guangdong

fǔ 【府】 prefecture

Fúdé Temple 【福德祠】 The oldest Chinese temple in Singapore. It was built in 1824 by Yuè and Kèjiā migrants and dedicated to Dàbó Gōng.

Fúqīng xiàn 【福清县】 former Fúqīng county in Fúzhōu prefecture. Now Fúqīng city

Fúzhōu fǔ 【福州府】 a former prefecture in Fujian province.

Fujian shěng 【福建省】 Fujian province

Fuk Tak Chi (Yuèhǎi) 【福德祠】 see Fú-dé Temple

Fúlǎo 【福佬】 Mǐnnán people from Fujian Province and Taiwan

ga-gi-nang (Cháoshàn) 【家己侬】 those on our side (literal translation: one of the family)

Gan Eng Seng (Fúlǎo) School 【颜永成学校】 pronounced as Yán Yǒng Chéng School in Mandarin

Gàn yǔ 【赣语】 Gàn language

gāo-zú 【高卒】 In Chinese chess, refers to a pawn that has only reached the opponent's pawn rank.

Geok Hong Tian (Fúlǎo) 【玉皇殿】 see Yùhuáng Diàn

Ghee Hin (Fúlǎo) Company 【义兴公司】 see Yìxīng

Ghee Hock (Fúlǎo) Company 【义福公司】 see Yìfú

gōngsī 【公司】 business company, firm, corporation

guā-kang-lâng (Fúlǎo) 【外江侬】 Mǐnnán word to describe a northerner (or person from North China)

guānxi 【关系】 a Chinese social concept based on the exchange of favors, placing more importance on personal relationships than laws and written agreements.

Guǎnbǎo 【莞宝】 a Cantonese dialect

Guǎng Hǎi Shān 【广海山】 the Yuè branch of the Hǎi Shān Society

Guǎngdōng 【广东】 a province in south China

Guǎngfǔ 【广府】 Cantonese language

Guǎngzhōu 【广州】 the capital and largest city of Guangdong province, People's Republic of China.

Guǎngzhōu fǔ 【广州府】 a former prefecture in Guangdong province.

Guānhuà 【官话】 the language of high government officials (Mandarin)

Guānhuà 【官话】 language of the officials

Gugang district 【古冈州】 known as Xinhui district today

Guó-mín-bào 【国民报】 a newspaper founded by the Guomindang under the leadership of Sun Yat-sen and Chen Xinzheng in 1914,

Guóyǔ 【国语】 National Language (Mandarin)

Gwong-dung (Yuèhǎi) 【广东】 see Guǎngdōng

Gwong-fu (Yuèhǎi) 【广府】 see Guǎngfǔ

Gwong-zau (Yuèhǎi) 【广州】 see Guǎngzhōu

Gwong-zau-fu (Yuèhǎi) 【广州府】 see Guǎngzhōu fǔ

Hai San (Fúlǎo) Company 【海山公司】 see Hǎi Shān

Hǎishān Company 【海山公司】 secret society that was allied
    with the Jiàndé Society in Penang. (also known as wǔ-xiàn)

Hǎiyáng 【海阳】 ancient name for Cháo'ān

Hakka (Kèjiā) 【客家】 see Kèjiā

hángshāng 【行商】 A liaison between foreign traders and the
    Chinese. Because the license to trade was monopolistic,
    these liaison wielded much power.

Héhé shè 【和合社】 a Penang-based triad, members were mi-
    grants from Xinning.

Henghua (Fúlǎo) Army 【兴化军】 see Xīnghuà Army

Ho Hap Seah (Yuèhǎi) 【和合社】 see Héhé Shè

Hokchew hu (Fúlǎo) 【福州府】 see Fúzhōu fǔ

Hokchia kuan (Fúlǎo) 【福清县】 see Fúqīng xiàn

Hokkien síng (Fúlǎo) 【福建省】 see Fujian shěng

Hoklo (Fúlǎo) 【福佬】 see Fúlǎo

hong (Yuèhǎi) merchants 【行商】 see hángshāng

Hóng Wén School 【宏文学校】 a primary school

Hóngbīng 【洪兵】 great army

Hóngbīng 【红兵】 red army

Hongsun (Cháoshàn) 【丰顺】 see Fēngshùn

hú (Fúlǎo) 【府】 see fǔ

huà 【话】 dialect / spoken language

Huájīxì 【滑稽戏】 Shanghai farce opera, started in the early twen-
    tieth century.

Huáshēng Society 【华生会】 a Kèjiā triad in Penang

Huáinán 【淮南】 a prefecture-level city in central Anhui Province

Huat Chu Kong (Fúlǎo) 【法主公】 see Fǎ Zhǔgōng

huay kuan (Fúlǎo) 【会馆】 see huìguǎn

huay kwan (Fúlǎo) 【会馆】 see huìguǎn

huì 【会】 union, group, or association

huìguǎn 【会馆】 provincial or prefectural or county guild hall

Huìzhōu fǔ 【惠州府】 a former prefecture in Guangdong province.

Hui'an Xiàn 【惠安县】 Formerly Hui'an county in Quánzhōu prefecture. Now Hui'an city

Jiàndé Society 【建德会】 secret society that was allied with the Hǎi Shān Society in Penang. Its members were of Zhangzhou ancestry.

jiǎng-huáyǔ-yùndòng 【讲华语运动】 a campaign to encourage Singaporean Chinese to speak Mandarin rather than other Chinese languages.

Jiānghuái Guānhuà 【江淮官话】 Lower Yangtze subvariety of Mandarin

Jiāngnán 【江南】 south of Changjiang or Yangtze river / south of the lower reaches of Changjiang / often refers to south Jiangsu, south Anhui and north Zhejiang provinces / a province during early Qing times

Jiāngzhè 【江浙】 abbr. for Jiangsu and Zhejiang Provinces during late Qing times

Jiēyáng 【揭阳】 During Qing dynasty, a district in Chaozhou Prefecture, Guangdong Province

Jìnjiāng Xiàn 【晋江县】 former Jìnjiāng county in Quánzhōu prefecture. Now Jìnjiāng city

Jīnmén Xiàn 【金门县】 former Jīnmén county in Quánzhōu prefecture. Now Kinmen County, Taiwan

Jinan Academy 【暨南学堂】

Jinan National University 【国立暨南大学】

Jīnhuā 【金花】 Lady Golden Flower is believed to grant the wishes of her worshiper's generations of descendants.

jyut (Yuèhǎi) 【粤】 see Yuè

jyut-hoi (Yuèhǎi) 【粤海】 see Yuèhǎi

jyut-jyu (Yuèhǎi) 【粤语】 see Yuèyǔ

Kam Fa (Yuèhǎi) 【金花】 see Jīnhuā

kán (Fúlǎo) 【嫺】 This character is not listed in many Chinese character dictionaries. It is a Mǐnnán character meaning enslaved servant girl.

Kèjiā 【客家】 a variety of Chinese language spoken in southern China and Taiwan.

Khee Fatt (Kèjiā) School 【启发小学】 see Qifa School

Khek (Fúlǎo) 【客】 see Kèjiā

Kian Tek (Fúlǎo) Society 【建德会】 see Jiàndé Society

Kok Min Pao 【国民报】 see Guó-mín-bào

kongsi (Fúlǎo) 【公司】 see gōngsī

Kūnqǔ 【昆曲】 influential musical theater originating in Kunshan, Jiangsu province in the Yuan dynasty.

Kwong-fu (Yuèhǎi) 【广府】 see Guǎngfǔ

Kwong Hai San (Fúlǎo) 【广海山】 see Guǎng Hǎi Shān

Lam Ann Kuan (Fúlǎo) 【南安县】 see Nan'an Xiàn

lǎoshī 【老师】 teacher

lau-kuah-sae-ngah (Shanghainese) 【老刮三额】 Shanghainese expression for weird.

leung t'au sha (Yuèhǎi) 【两头蛇】 double-headed snake

lǐ 【里】 Chinese mile (approx. 537–645 meters)

Lord Chénghuáng 【城隍爷】 A daoist deity

Lǔ Xùn 【鲁迅】 a leading figure of modern Chinese literature.

mǎ 【马】 Horse

Māzǔ 【妈祖】 the Chinese goddess of the sea who is said to protect fishermen and sailors.

Min Yuen 【民运】 Romanization used in British Malaya. see mínyùn.

Mǐn yǔ 【闽语】 Min language, spoken in parts of Fujian and Guangdong Province, Taiwan etc.

Mǐn Dōng 【闽东】 Literal: east Fujian. Refers to a subvariety of the Mǐn language

Mǐnnán 【闽南】 Literal: south Fujian. Refers to a subvariety of the Mǐn language

mòxiěbǐsài 【默写比赛】 Chinese-language recitation and dictation competition.

muē-á (Fúlǎo) 【妹仔】 variant pronunciation for bē-á.

mui-tsai (Yuèhǎi) 【妹仔】 term used in sex traffic. (see also bē-á)

Nam Việt (Vietnamese) 【-】 see Nányuè

Nan'an Xiàn 【南安县】 former Nan'an county in Quánzhōu prefecture. Now Nan'an city

Nándà 【南大】 an abbreviation for Nányáng Dàxué

Nantah 【南大】 see Nándà

Nányáng 【南洋】 Literal: South Seas. Meaning: Southeast Asia.

Nányáng Dàxué 【南洋大学】 Nanyang University

Nányuè 【南越】 an ancient kingdom occupying much of what is now northern Vietnam and the southern Chinese provinces of Kwangtung and Kwangsi.

Ngee Heng (Cháoshàn) 【义兴】 see Yì Xīng

ngo-kuān (Fúlǎo) 【五县】 see wǔ-xiàn

ni-hein (Taishanese) 【义兴】 see Yì Xīng

nou-pei (Yuèhǎi) 【奴婢】 enslaved servant girl. (see also núbì)

nú-bì 【奴婢】 enslaved servant girl. (see also nou pei)

Nyonya (Malay) 【-】 a term used by the Malays, referring to the Straits-Chinese women.

péidú māmā 【陪读妈妈】 Mothers who accompany their children studying in Singapore.

Peranakan (Malay) Chinese 【-】 a term used for the descendants of the 15th through 17th-century Chinese immigrants to the Indonesian archipelago and British Malaya.

Ping Ming [sic] Reading Room 【平民书报社】 see Píngmín Reading Room

Píngmín Reading Room 【平民书报社】 a reading room

Poh Leung Kuk (Yuèhǎi) 【保良局】 Society for the Protection of Women and Children

Poit-ip (Cháoshàn) 【八邑】 eight districts

Pútián xiàn 【莆田县】 former Pútián county in Quánzhōu prefecture.

pǔtōnghuà 【普通话】 ordinary speech or modern standard language rather than classical Chinese

Punti (Taishanese) 【本地】 see běndì

Púxiān huà 【莆仙话】 a dialect of Mǐnnán

Qifa School 【启发小学】 known as Qifa Primary School today

Qin Guan 【秦观】 Chinese writer and poet of the Song Dynasty. His courtesy name was Shaoyou or Taixu. His pseudonym was Huaihai Jushi and Hangou Jushi.

Qīngyuǎn xiàn 【清远县】 former Qīngyuǎn county in Guǎngzhōu prefecture. Now a prefecture-level city in Guangdong province.

Qīng-yuán-zhēn-jūn Temple 【清元真君庙】 Temple in Singapore for migrants from Changtai county, Zhangzhou. Now defunct.

Quánzhōu fǔ 【泉州府】 Quánzhōu prefecture

Quemoy Kuan (Fúlǎo) 【金门县】 see Jīnmén Xiàn

Róufú Gǔmiào 【柔佛古廟】 Johor Bahru Old Chinese Temple

saang seng waa (Yuèhǎi) 【省城话】 see shěngchéng huà

Sai Kwan (Yuèhǎi) 【西关】 see Xiguan

sài-xiàng-yǎn 【塞象眼】 Block the elephant's eye, a tactical move in Chinese chess.

sai-gong (Yuèhǎi) 【西江】 West River in Guangdong Province

sai-lou-neoi (Yuèhǎi) 【细路女】 young girl.

Sam Kiang 【三江】 see Sānjiāng

Samsui (Yuèhǎi) 【三水】 see Sānshuǐ

Samyap (Yuèhǎi) 【三邑】 see Sānyì

Sānshuǐ 【三水】 a district in Foshan, Guangdong province, China

Sānjiāng 【三江】 literally "three rivers"

Sānjiāng Kǒu 【三江口】 Ningpo's central Y-shaped river confluence

Sānyì 【三邑】 the three former counties of Panyu, Nanhai, and
Shunde

see-kuan (Fúlǎo) 【四县】 see sì-xiàn

Shantou 【汕头】 prefecture level city in Guangdong

shè 【社】 society, group, club, or agency

shěng 【省】 provinces

shěngchéng huà 【省城话】 Language of the provincial capital
(Cantonese language)

Sǐhǎi Huá Yí Zǒngtú 【四海华夷总图】 literally: "World Diagram
of China and the Barbarians." It is a Chinese world map,
dated 1532, now located at the Harvard Library.

sì-xiàn 【四县】 four counties

Sìyì 【四邑】 the four former counties of Xinhui, Taishan, Kaiping
and Enping (Taishanese is the most prominent dialect of the
Sìyì language.)

Sin Chew (Fúlǎo) Reading Room 【星洲书报社】 see Xīngzhōu
Reading Room

Su Shi 【苏轼】 Chinese writer, poet, painter, calligrapher, phar-
macologist, gastronome, and a statesman of the Song Dynasty.

Swatow (Fúlǎo) 【汕头】 see Shantou

Sze Yap (Yuèhǎi) 【四邑】 see Sìyì

Tai Pu (Kèjiā) 【大埔】 See Dabu

taipan (Yuèhǎi) 【大班】 foreign business manager

Tái-Xià Dào 【台厦道】 Taiwan-Xiamen Defense Region, established by the Kangxi Emperor

Tao Nan School (Wade-Giles) 【道南学校】 a Special Assistance
Plan (SAP) primary school

Teochew hu (Fúlǎo) 【潮州府】 see Chaozhou fǔ

Thian Hock Keng (Fúlǎo) Temple 【天福宫】 see Tiān-fǔ-gōng
Temple

Tiān-fǔ-gōng Temple 【天福宫】 Temple in Singapore for migrants from Haicheng county, Zhangzhou.

Tiāndìhuì 【天地会】 lit. Heaven and Earth Society; a Chinese fraternal organization

Tiānjīng 【天京】 "Heavenly Capital" is the name given to Nanjing by Hong Xiuquan, king of the "Heavenly Kingdom of the Great Peace", during the Taiping Rebellion, in imperial China, from 1853 to 1864.

Toh Lam School (Fúlǎo) 【道南学校】 see Tao Nan School.

Tóng'ān Xiàn 【同安县】 former Tong'an county of Quánzhōu prefecture, now Tong'an district of Xiamen city.

Tóngdé Reading Room 【同德书报社】 a reading room

Tòngwén Reading Room 【同文书报社】 a reading room

towkay (Fúlǎo) 【头家】 a business owner; boss.

Tsa Bóo Kán (Fúlǎo) 【查某嫺】 female kán, a variant of kán. see kán, especially if the Chinese character did not display.

Tsaú Kán (Fúlǎo) 【查某嫺】 variant Mǐnnán pronunciation for Tsa Bóo Kán.

Tua-pek Kong (Fúlǎo) 【大伯公】 see Dàbó Gōng

tuan besar (Malay) 【-】 a European boss in colonial Malaya

Tuan Mong (Cháoshàn) School 【端蒙学校】 see Duanmeng School

Tung Ann Kuan (Fúlǎo) 【同安县】 see Tóng'ān xiàn

Tung Teh (Cháoshàn) Reading Room 【同德书报社】 see Tóngdé Reading Room

Tung Wen (Hainanese) Reading Room 【同文书报社】 see Tòngwén Reading Room

Wah Sang (Kèjiā) 【华生会】 see huáshēng

Wak Hai Cheng Bio (Cháoshàn) 【粤海清庙】 see Yuè-hǎi-qīng Temple

Wang Chaoyun 【王朝云】 concubine of Su Shi

wéiqí 【围棋】 a strategic board game for two players.

Wénchāng Dìjūn 【文昌帝君】 the God of Culture and Literature

wǔ-xiàn 【五县】 five counties

wǔyī 【五邑】 five districts from four counties, Taishan, Kaiping, Enping, and Heshan

Wǔdài Shíguó 【五代十国】 was an era of political upheaval in China from 907–960/979 AD, between the fall of the Tang Dynasty and the founding of the Song Dynasty.

Wúyuè 【吴越】 an independent coastal kingdom (907-979 CE) during the Five Dynasties and Ten Kingdoms of Chinese history.

xīnán guānhuà 【西南官话】 Southwestern subvariety of Mandarin

Xiàmén 【厦门】 city in Fujian

xiàn 【县】 county

Xiānyóu xiàn 【仙游县】 former Xiānyóu county in Quánzhōu prefecture. Now Xiānyóu county in Pútián

xiǎo-nǚ-hái 【小女孩】 young girl.

Xiguan 【西关】 Former name of Liwan District, Guangzhou.

Xīnghuà Army 【兴化军】 an army garrisoned in Fujian Province during the Song Dynasty.

Xinning County 【新宁县】 known as Taishan (Toisan) City today.

Xīngzhōu Reading Room 【星洲书报社】 a reading room

xùbì 【蓄婢】 enslaved servant girl.

Xuánwǔ 【玄武】 lit. "Dark Warrior." It is the name of a high-ranked Daoist deity who is particularly revered by martial artists.

yánhǎi qiānjiè 【沿海迁界】 Kangxi Emperor ordered the evacuation of the coastal areas of Guangdong in order to fight the anti-Qing movement. The provinces of Shandong, Zhejiang, Jiangsu and Fujian were also affected to varying degrees.

Yangzheng School 【养正学校】 A school founded in 1905, for Yuèhǎi children. It is known as Yangzheng Primary School today

Yeung Ching (Yuèhǎi) School 【养正学校】 see Yangzheng School

Yìfú Company 【义福公司】 a Secret Society in Singapore.

Yìxīng Company 【义兴公司】 a Secret Society in Malaya.

Yin Sin (Kèjiā) School 【应新学校】 see Yingxin School

Yingxin School 【应新学校】 now defunct

Yoke Eng (Hainanese) School 【育英学校】 see Yuying School

Yǒngchūn Zhílìzhōu 【永春直隶州】 Yǒngchūn directly administrated department

Yǒngdìng 【永定】 During Qing dynasty, a county in Tingzhou Prefecture, Fujian Province

Yǔ Gòng 【禹贡】 Tribute of Yu: one of the Five Classics of ancient Chinese literature.

Yùhuáng Diàn 【玉皇殿】 Temple of Jade Emperor

Yuè 【粤】 Cantonese

Yuè-hǎi-qīng Temple 【粤海清庙】 a Chinese temple in Singapore

Yuegang 【月港】 Literal: Moon Harbor

Yuèhǎi 【粤海】 Cantonese

yuèjì 【粤妓】 Yuè prostitutes.

Yuèjù 【越剧】 Shaoxing opera. Shaoxing is a dialect spoken in
Zhejiang

Yuèyǔ 【粤语】 Cantonese language

Yuèzhōngbùchánzúhuì 【粤中不缠足会】 Canton [sic Yuè] Foot
Emancipation Society

Yuying School 【育英学校】 known as Yuying Primary School today

Zhānglín Gǔgǎng 【樟林古港】 Old Port of Zhānglín

Zhāngzhōu fǔ 【漳州府】 Zhāngzhōu prefecture

Zhàoqìng fǔ 【肇庆府】 formerly a prefecture in Guangdong province.

Zhìtóng Reading Room 【志同书报社】 a reading room

zhílìzhōu 【直隶州】 directly administrated department

Zhōngshān 【中山】 a Cantonese dialect

Zhōngyuán Guānhuà 【中原官话】 Central Plains Mandarin, a subvariety of Mandarin

zhōu 【州】 a territorial unit

zú 【卒】 soldier or pawn in Chinese chess

###